REPUBLIC OF TEXAS. Vol.

nts shall Come, Know ye

T of the Republic aforesaid, by virtue of the power vested in me by **LAW**, and in a

T to *Theodore Bennett his* _____

er of his headright

the San Jacinto, Beginning at the South west corner of H. b

at 70 varas distant and a Red Oak, 24 in. dia. mkd F C bear

her a post from which a Pine, 11 in. dia. mkd W. 8 bear S 50

nts, thence North one thousand varas to South East co

dia. mkd X bears S 65 W. 4 varas distant and another Red

with South boundary of said survey one thousand varas

a Stake from which a Red Oak, 10 in. dia. mkd X b

bears N 30 W. 3 varas distant, thence South with

nd *his* heirs or assigns, **FOREVER,** all the right and title in and to said **LAND,**

nt for the same.

Great Seal of the REPUBLIC *to be affixed as well as the Seal of the* GENERAL LAND O

DONE at the *City of Austin* _____

the _____ *day of September one thousand*

hundred and forty-four and the year of the Independence of said Rep

the Ninth _____

President

MONTGOMERY COUNTY, TEXAS

PICTURE OF A DREAM COMING TRUE

Written by Dr. Margaret A. Simpson
On Behalf of the Heritage Museum

THE
DONNING COMPANY
PUBLISHERS

The Donning Company/Publishers
184 Business Park Drive, Suite 106
Virginia Beach, VA 23462

Steve Mull, General Manager
Barbara A. Bolton, Project Director
Tracey Emmons-Schneider, Director of Research
Sally C. Wise, Editor
Joseph C. Schnellmann, Graphic Designer
Dawn V. Kofroth, Assistant General Manager
Tony Lillis, Director of Marketing
Teri S. Arnold, Marketing Coordinator

Cataloging-in-Publication   Data:

Simpson, Margaret, 1935-
        Montgomery County, Texas : picture of a dream coming true
Margaret A. Simpson
                        p.   cm.
        Photographs from the collection of the Heritage
  Museum of Montgomery County
        Includes bibliographical references (p.   ) and index.
        ISBN 0-89865-997-3
        1. Montgomery County (Tex.)—History—Pictorial works.
I. Heritage Museum of Montgomery County (Conroe, Tex.) II. Title.
F392.M7S56   1997
976.4'153—dc21   97-10442
                                                  CIP

Printed in the United States of America

TABLE OF CONTENTS

I know a person here who totally embodies the Dream of Montgomery County. She is full of knowledge about our past, actively involved in keeping that past alive for the present generation, and enthusiastically devoted to preserving it for the future. In her presence history comes alive. Our forefathers become real people whose life-fabric is very much like our own. She works most creatively to let our children experience and appreciate the life of the early county.

My knowledge of and love for this place have been incredibly enriched and vitalized because of her and with deep admiration and gratitude, I dedicate this book to Gertie Weisinger Spencer, the Curator of the Heritage Museum.

Even as a child Gertie and her brother Louis (Bubba) learned the value of tradition. She's sitting in a chair made for her mother in 1907. Gertie's children and her grandchildren have all used this chair.

A C K N O W L E D G M E N T S

T hanks to the Board of the Heritage Museum for having the love of our history that led them to conceive of this project, to our generous underwriters who understand that today's successes are in part a result of yesterday's achievements, to all those who shared their memories in photographs, to our photographer, David Hopper, and to these printed sources:

W. H. Gandy's Thesis *A History of Montgomery County, Texas* (1952)

Robin Montgomery's *The History of Montgomery County* (1975); Jenkins Publishing Company, Pemberton Press; Austin

Montgomery County Genealogical Society's *Montgomery County History* (1981)

Celeste Graves'*Magnolia Memories,* Self-published (1993).

These volumes and many more memoirs and documents are part of the museum archives and are available to all of you for further study. All unattributed photographs are from the collection of the Heritage Museum.

The Dream That Drew Them

Moses Austin's sense of the dynamic future of Texas became his son's dream. His father had secured permission to settle three hundred families in this large area and in 1821 when Moses Austin died, Stephen Austin took over the plan.

The area had been largely ignored before this. The first record of it is in a log of the French explorer LaSalle who passed through here in 1686 but he was actually lost at the time! However, this mention of French presence triggered the Spanish (rivals of the French) interest here. A Spanish expedition was sent and in its retinue was a priest, a Father Massenet, who established a number of missions. The early road from the Goliad Mission to the Nacogdoches Mission went through what would later become

Although the Baudat family did not reach Montgomery County until 1910, their story reflects the determination of many who came. Joseph and Celeste sailed from France in 1880. They had four young children and spoke no English. After a near sinking of their ship they arrived in Nova Scotia and took a train to Texas living first in Weatherford and later in Montgomery County. (Courtesy of Celeste Graves)

No.

El Ciudadano ESTEVAN F. AUSTIN, Empresario, para introducir Emigrados Estrangeros, en las Colonias que le tiene designadas el Supremo Gobierno del Estado de Coahuila y Texas, por los contratos celebrados entre el dicho Gobierno y el mismo Austin, al efecto:

CERTIFICO, Que *Mary Corner* es uno de los Colonos, que he introducido en virtud de mis contratos antes mencionados; que llego en esta Colonia el dia _____ del mes de *diciembre*, del año de 18 *29*; que es *viuda*, y consta su familia de *cuatro* personas, segun la declaracion que me ha presentado, firmada por él mismo: y me consta, que ha prestado, ante el Alcalde, el juramento que previene el articulo tercero de la Ley de Colonizacion del Estado.

· Doy esta certificacion al dicho *Mary Corner* para presentar al Señor Comisionado, nombrado por el Gobierno para rapartir tierras y espedir titulos: como constancia que entra en mis referidos contratos.

Quedara nulo este documento, si el interesado no se presenta al dicho Comisionado con este, dentro de un mes, despues de publicarse en esta, un aviso publico al efecto, igualmente quedara nulo, se pareciese que la dicha declaracion hecha por el intersado, es falsa, en cualquiera parte; o si el mismo sale de esta Colonia, antes de recibir su titulo de posecion, a establecerse en otro punto; o si no cumple con las condiciones de pago, espresadas en el aviso publico, publicado por mi con fecha 20 be Noviembre de 1829, sobre la materia, y manifestado al interesado al tiempo de entregarse este.

VILLA DE AUSTIN, *19* de *Marzo* de 18 *30*.

Estevan F. Austin

por Samuel M. W...

This document issued to Mary Corner on March 19, 1830 was a letter from Stephen Austin to "introduce foreign immigrants in the colonies designated by the state of Coahuila and Texas." A widow, she arrived in December 1829 with her four children, a typical early settler of Texas drawn by the dream of land and new beginnings.

Montgomery County. This ushered in a brief period of Spanish activity but no real colonization of the area, and the planned mission at Spring Creek was soon abandoned.

It was Austin, though, who made the dream accessible to the people. From the legislature of Coahuila and Texas came a colonization law which offered land grants to aspiring farmers. One version of the grant package suggests that a married man might have been offered 177 acres (known as a *labor*). If he also wanted to raise cattle he could receive as much as 4,215 acres. Each *labor* cost $3.50 if irrigable and $2.50 if not. If a person wanted both farm land and cattle land for a total of twenty five *labores*, his combined cost would have been $30 with six years to pay it off. (Sounds like a real bargain to those buying land in Montgomery County today!) Of course an unmarried man could get only one-fourth this much. Our founding fathers certainly knew how to encourage family values!

Although others also received land grants in this area, including Hayden Edwards and Joseph Verlein, it was Austin's colony that became the center of civilization here. Some forty-two families received land titles and the dynamic life of our county began. General A. B. Wheeler, an officer in the U.S. Army, so believed in the potential of Texas that in 1923 he resigned his commission, accepted one of Austin's land grants and moved here. From the prosperity of a Virginia planter's life, he brought his wife and two small children to what would be Montgomery County. When he arrived he hand-built a log cabin, dug a well for a supply of water, and planted crops for food. No one lived

Julius Jefferson, veteran of the Confederate Army, brought his wife Sarah to Galveston by boat and then to Old Danville in 1872. Three small children and Sarah's mother accompanied them. Imagine a slow boat ride from Georgia to Galveston with three babies and a mother-in-law. Those early settlers had "true grit." (Courtesy of Celeste Graves)

within forty miles so he offered one hundred acres of his land to any new settlers "of good moral character" and through this offer he acquired neighbors. He suffered an early Indian attack, the loss of a son to malaria, and a fire which destroyed his original cabin but he endured, sustained by his dream of Texas' future. He must have passed his vision on to his family as well, for one of his grandsons was Price Daniel, a governor of Texas.

Eventually many others followed. Who came? Mostly settlers from the South: Georgia, Alabama, and Mississippi. They began arriving on long wagon trains by 1830 and by May of 1831, thirty grants had been issued. They brought with them household goods, slaves in some cases, and the burning determination to create a civilization here, to seize the opportunity to plant, to produce, and to prosper. They were not soft people, not always refined. But look in their eyes as you gaze at these pictures and you will see strength and courage aplenty.

When the settlers did arrive, they found very few amenities. There were Indians in the area, the Kickapoos and the Bedias. Fortunately, they were rather peaceful. Camping around Spring Creek and Caney Creek, they traded with the newcomers, bringing baskets, rattan and hickory goods, bowls, and other storage vessels. The Indians' impact here was minimal because they were all but irradicated in early fever epidemics.

These "pioneers" built houses, furnishing them with precious treasures brought from home and then went to work on their newly acquired land. Supplies had to be brought in from fifty miles away and for the most part they lived off the land, enjoying honey, fish, and wild game. Mother Nature offered much here: fertile soil, timber of all sorts, fruit for picking (berries, grapes, pecans, and persimmons), flowers (jasmine, dogwood, and magnolia), fish (in open, unpolluted creeks and rivers) and game. Such early place names as Panther Creek and Bear Bend remind us of those days.

The influx and industry of those early settlers led W.W. Shepherd to say in 1837, "It is expected that a new county will be organized ... embracing this section of the country." The bill to create this new county was introduced on November 23 and signed by Sam Houston on December 14, 1837. Montgomery County thus became the third county in Texas. At that time, this county included large parts of present-day Grimes, Walker, Waller, San Jacinto, and Madison Counties and did not take on its current size of 1,017 square miles until 1873. Although lessening in size over these early years, the county lost none of its vitality. These people created towns, governments, built buildings, churches, and schools. They worked first in farming, then in timber and on railroads, and finally in oil fields to keep a flourishing economy. They valued the freedom they enjoyed, worked diligently to keep it, and also found time for fun. In these pages, we have tried to recreate for you what life was like in Montgomery County from 1830 until World War II.

Share this insight and then you will see why those of us who still live here very much share that legacy and carry with us our own version of the dream that drew them!

After the death of her husband Jacob, Caroline Lafitte Strozier came to Willis in 1867 to live with her son August. She brought two daughters, Fadonia and Lula, and a son Jacob, Jr. Although the picture (from an old ambrotype) is cracked, her strength clearly shows! (Courtesy of Rosamond Stewart)

James Samuel Stewart

son of

William Stewart and Eliza Childs

James Samuel Stewart and his second wife, Mary Eliza O'Bannion, came here from South Carolina in the mid-1850s and settled on a land grant between Willis and Montgomery. (Courtesy of Rosamond Stewart)

Left: William Landrum applied for a land grant before 1830. When he received one between Lake Creek and Atkins Creek (west of Dobbin), he came here from South Carolina, settled the land, survived the early rigors and served the county as Constable of Precinct Three in 1878. (Courtesy of Anna Weisinger)

Right: Lemuel Clepper, like most of the early settlers, received his land grant (640 acres) and settled here in 1837. He farmed his own land, was listed in the 1860 census as a dentist and served the county as District Clerk, Justice of the Peace, Sheriff, and County Commissioner. Wonder what he did in his spare time? (Courtesy of Celeste Graves)

Lizzie Thomas Brister's parents, John and Phoebe Thomas, early land grant settlers, gave far more than they got. One brother died at the Alamo and another at San Jacinto. Lizzie was born in a log house, lived there all her life, and died there at the age of 108. I'll bet she had cooked all that food on the table by herself. Those early settlers were not weak! (Courtesy of Dortha Altman)

Annie Howard's life span (1832–1916)
is that of our seminal growth period.
The women, like the men, built this
county with strength, a deep faith and
great endurance.

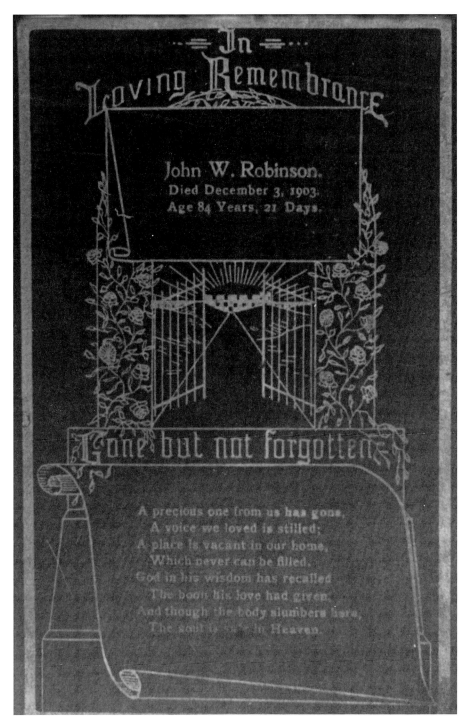

Unlike most who came to plant, John W. Robinson saw that the county needed other services as well. He and his wife Louisa ran a boarding house in New Caney. When he died in 1908, many who had not been invited to the elegance of Elmwood and Esperanza probably grieved for a genial host.

The old Crawford home in Willis was actually built by Capt. Thomas Wesley Smith in 1872. Smith was a merchant, a civil servant (sheriff at only twenty-one!) and a captain in the Confederate Army. Smith also built an Opera House in Willis. His daughter Margaret later married Judge S. A. Crawford. The home features the wide verandahs, the windows and fireplaces so typical of fine Montgomery County homes in the nineteenth century. Unfortunately the house burned in 1964.

Not everyone enjoyed the amenities of Elmwood and Esperanza. A far more typical home is the old log cabin built by Jeptha Muckle near Dobbin. He came here, *paid for his land* rather than receiving a grant, and built this sturdy home with wooden shingles and a single door. Originally a corn crib, it was also a home in which Papa Tharp was born in 1849. Time may ravage roofs but not the vision our forefathers brought here. (Courtesy of Bessie Owen)

Elmwood, built on the Lewis plantation near Willis, was a stately, gracious house equal to the finest in the Deep South, complete with columns, moss-hung trees, and rolling lawns. John Lewis used slaves brought from Virginia to build this three story house out of bricks imported from Holland and native timber from twenty sawmills. It took them two full years to complete.

In 1879 William F. Spiller had high hopes for his tobacco plantation. Thus he chose to name his home Esperanza meaning "Hope!" The home, a sixteen-room mansion constructed in the Virginia style and built on Shepherd Hill Road, outlasted the business.

Giving Dimensions to the Dream

The dream of these early settlers drew them here and sustained them but their energy and industry relied also on leaders who gave that dream direction and dimension both locally and at the state level. There were many such leaders but none so central to the future of Montgomery County as Dr. Charles Bellinger Stewart.

Dr. Stewart came here in 1831 from South Carolina to practice his profession—medicine—and it was here that he met and married Julia Shepherd. Although he had plenty to do in the area near Montgomery where his family settled and built a home, Dr. Stewart also served in the Army of the Republic of Texas as interpreter between Sam Houston and Santa Anna. Later, he served on the committee to draft our state constitution and was Texas' first secretary of state. Artist as well as healer, soldier, and statesman, he designed our State Seal and created our state's proud Lone Star Flag.

After fighting in the Civil War, J. L. Turner and his wife Lydia came here by wagon train. The first animal they saw on their new land was a mink—hence Mink's Prairie became a part of Montgomery County history. (Courtesy of Celeste Graves)

Dr. C. B. Stewart (1806–1885) was a founding father of this county and a major contributor to the creation of Texas. His kind eyes do not suggest softness but that of a vision and determination. He was one of the first signers of the Texas Declaration of Independence, fought to make it true, served as our first Secretary of State, and designed both our state seal and the Lone Star Flag.

The modest proportions and the bare barbed wire of this home built in 1840 do not truly reflect the richness of the owner's contribution to the state and to this county. Dr. Charles B. Stewart came here in 1831 and is buried in the old Montgomery Cemetery.

The county itself drew its name from the earliest major center—the community of Montgomery. It was here that Owen Shannon established a trading post on Town Creek around 1830. He named it Montgomery after his wife Margaret Montgomery whose father, William Montgomery, had come to Texas in 1820 as a surveyor and moved here permanently in the early 1830s. With the expanding community, the trading post was a natural magnet and gathering place for the townspeople. In 1838, the W. W. Shepherd home was purchased for $800 to be used as a courthouse. All was not perfect in this young township, for the very next civic project was the purchase of a building to be used as the jail!

As a county seat, the town of Montgomery prospered. Another early leader, Dr. James H. Price, showed us the versatility of our first citizens. He came to Montgomery County in 1839 to practice medicine with Dr. E. J. Arnold, who had settled here in 1836. Both men were active in civic life and Dr. Price was a farmer and trader as well. He built a grist mill and a gin to support his own farm as well as those of his neighbors. The town's growth drew many more entrepreneurs such as the Willis brothers, Peter J. and Richard, who opened a general store under the name Cawthon, Willis and Bro.

Montgomery remained a thriving community described by a visitor as a village containing many tasty residences until the Civil War. Then new growth spurred by the railroad brought the community of Willis into prominence around 1870. The town was named by the railroad after the Willis brothers of Montgomery but no loyalty seemed to exist, for a rivalry sprang up between the two towns as to which would be the county seat. In 1874 Willis received that title and many businesses moved there. A major building boom began in the 1890s due to the tobacco industry there but when that market waned, timber replaced it, occasioning the stimulus of yet another town—Conroe.

Dr. James H. Price first came to Houston to practice medicine but in 1842, noting in his diary that Houston was "a cut-throat place, no medicine, no office and not one friend," he purchased land here. In the next forty years he became a central figure in the community. For example, he was part of a group of business men who established a railroad with lines running from Montgomery to Navasota. (Courtesy of Bessie Owen)

Left: Dr. Price's wife Elizabeth Ann Morgan had come here from Scotland and was noted for "her industrious Manner." Since she had run a boarding house in Scotland, Dr. Price built one for her here—the acclaimed Price's Hotel. (Courtesy of Bessie Owen)
Right: Morgan L. Price, son of Elizabeth and Dr. Price, went through the Civil War then studied medicine at Tulane. This photo was taken in 1869. (Courtesy of Bessie Owen)

Jacob Montgomery Shannon, the son of Owen Shannon, shows the same determination and strength of his parents. He had been an Indian trader but moved here after the Fredonia Rebellion. At his death, he deeded land next to his plantation home for a church, a school and a cemetery—the Jacob Shannon Evergreen Cemetery.

The "New" Cemetery, final resting place of Dr. Stewart as well as other notable leaders of the county, was located on a plot given by the Willis brothers in 1868. Note, however, that its first occupants were men killed by vigilantes. The county still needed some taming!

In January 1881 Isaac Conroe bought a tract of land and built a sawmill near the town of Beech in 1885. The railroad he used to travel on from Houston to check on his business made a stop here and called it Conroe's Switch. (We in Conroe are glad it later became simply Conroe!) By 1899 the town had about three hundred residents and on April 27, 1899, became the county seat (by only sixty-two votes!) The tale is told around here that that election was "swung" by a coalition of Willis and Conroe businessmen to prevent Montgomery from reclaiming rights to the courthouse. By 1900 Conroe boasted 1,009 residents. Its growth reflected that of the county. First, vitalized by the railroad; second,

Captain T. W. Smith, like so many Southerners, kept his military title after the Civil War. He came to Montgomery from Kentucky while still a boy of sixteen. Then seeing the new dynamics of the county, he moved his mercantile business to Willis as did many others—following the railroad!

Peter Willis got his first look at Texas in 1837 and went back to Maryland to persuade three of his brothers to join him here. After eighteen months, they purchased land and in 1843 opened a store in Montgomery. It flourished and expanded (even during the war). Following the war, the now prosperous brothers moved to Galveston becoming one of the largest mercantile houses in the West.

depending largely on timber, and third, receiving the tremendous stimulus of oil in 1931 which made the county rich and prosperous.

But to look at only these three towns would be deceiving, for in the early decades scores of communities sprang up, their names and fates reflecting the history of the county graphically. Many names simply record early settlers, scenic places, or memorials and little is known of them today. There

Although father Isaac gave the town its name, William Munger Conroe lived here, running the mill after his father's death and serving as post master. (Courtesy of Edmona Wooldridge Bowden)

Known as a "patriarch" of the town to some, Isaac Conroe set up a sawmill here near the end of the century. Since he rode the railroad (IG&N) from Houston to check on his mill, a railroad official established a regular stop here known as Conroe's Switch.

was Decker's Prairie, Grime's Prairie, Rayburn Chapel, McCrae, Hartley, and Morrisville. Grangerland, named after Don D. Granger, was heavily wooded and thinly populated with land being sold for $2 an acre. We have records of Hi-Point, Pleasant Grove, Bear Bend, Peach Creek, Turkey Creek, Lake Creek, and even Boggy Creek! The town of Waverley took its name from the novels of Sir Walter Scott and Longstreet from the renowned Civil War general.

Other names came into being because of the Post Office requirement that each name be unique. For example, Teddy (between Peach Creek and Turkey Creek) was first Eddy and it was here that fifty families took land grants arriving from Tennessee and Alabama in the 1860s. Later the Post Office changed its name to Teddy. That town is now deserted. The Robertson Settlement (1866) on the banks of Caney Creek had to be changed to New Caney because somewhere there was already a Caney. Cox's Switch, named for Charles Cox, took advantage of a new post office to become the town of Splendora in 1896, a name chosen for the splendor of its environment.

Several communities which once thrived have become ghost towns. Cinncinnati, the port on the Trinity River in the northeast part of the once larger county had over six hundred people in 1853 and even offered citizens a bowling alley! Then a sailor brought ashore yellow fever and within a few months the population was reduced to one hundred. By 1885, because of the Civil War blockades, there were only thirty five citizens and now it is simply gone. Before the Civil War, the town of Danville was home to 399 citizens, 600 slaves, a two teacher school and twelve businesses. Today it is only a remembered site.

The demise of some communities was clearly caused by economic pressures. Leonidas, site of the Trinity River Lumber Company mill once boasted a hotel, a grocery

Of course, any home site needed a well. Here, Frank Little, Sr., Frank, Jr., and friends are drilling such a well in North Conroe.
(Courtesy of Jo Walker)

29

Right: John Winston Wood arrived here with his father from Coffee County, Alabama shortly after the war. He married Mary Lindley and together they raised five children and farmed near Danville. (Courtesy of Rosamond Stewart.)

store, a train depot, and several two-story buildings. But when the mill shut down in 1924 everything vanished. A similar fate fell upon the town of Waukegan. In 1892 Waukegan was a prosperous lumber town with railroad access. Then the Depression led to its losing its schools and again there is only a signpost left as a reminder. Fostoria too, is only a sign on the railroad track and a cemetery. Originally Clinesburg, a mill town named for the mill's owner, it became Fostoria when the Foster Lumber Company bought the mill. The town was a true company town" whose 300-400 employees enjoyed many amenities such as free utilities, ice delivered from Conroe, and houses which rented for $1 per month per room! When the mill closed in 1957, so did the town. Dobbin, too, missed the wealth from the lumber mills. Originally Bobville, it became Dobbin in 1915 and knew some growth. (It had two hotels!) In 1916, the town tried digging for oil but the well turned out to be artesian water. Oh well, the spring still flows even if the town's hopes dried up.

Above and facing page: Samuel and Nancy Weisinger settled near Danville in the early 1840s. His ancestors were German brothers who had come to fight for the British in the Revolution but on seeing the promise of this new country, joined the Americans. This large clan had their own community Ryals, (close to what is April Sound today) where John, the oldest son, ran a general store and farmed 1,000 acres as well.

A sad reminder of the uncertainty of history, this marker hardly represents the hopes and endeavors of those who once farmed, shopped at Slanton's Store, and worshipped at the Catholic Church whose bell still stands in the yard. Betrayed by the railroad, Danville saw its businesses and most of its residents move to Willis.

The Robinson House on Danville St. in Willis (1910) with Mrs. Robinson and a friend at the gate. Mr. Robinson was versatile as many of our forefathers had to be. He farmed, owned a grocery store and a saloon. However, his wife refused to marry him until he gave up the saloon! She was Russ Clanton's mother-in-law. (Courtesy of Russ Clanton)

Some communities seemed to seek names which would create a positive image. We have already mentioned Splendora. Magnolia, originally Mink's Prairie, moved nearer the railroad in 1902 calling itself Melton for a local business man. When Mr. Melton left, the city renamed itself Magnolia for the stately trees abundant there at the time. The most impressive name in this category is surely Security. Originally named Bennette's Mill, the farming community was advertised in the North by the Security Land Company in 1910. Using exaggerated language and rigged pictures, promising wild oats shoulder high and fruited trees with opportunities to earn $10 a day picking them, the Company drew people here warning them not to associate with the natives, the old-timers. In 1912 these people came by train. One man brought fifty milk cows to feed on those wild oats! Most of these hapless folk went back home within the year. When the timber ran out and the mill closed, the entire town was deserted.

Early in the nineteenth century Jeptha Muckle came from England and purchased land east of Dobbin. There his daughter Mittie and her husband James M. Stinson built this home and raised four children. They owned the general store, the bank, the cotton gin and still found time to farm. Our forefathers weren't specialists!

When William Hoke gave his son Thomas Walter Hoke two hundred twenty acres near Bay's Chapel, he built his first home of hewn logs. Here two children were born. In 1870, Hoke remarried and built a two room house, eventually adding five bedrooms as his family grew. You can see the need for big houses in this picture.

J. F. Fisher, his wife and two daughters came to Old Waverley from Alabama in 1856. Emily married A. B. Strozier and lived at Brushy Creek. Another daughter married Dr. Oscar Tinsley the physician for Delta Land and Timber. All are buried in the old Waverley Cemetery. (Courtesy of Rosamond Stewart)

The home of John and Louisa Robinson in New Caney was not only a boarding house but a gathering place for locals, such as (left to right) E. Bonin, Charlie Freeman, Frank or Joe Presswood, Floy Sullivan, and Aunt Tennie. (Courtesy of Mrs. C. J. VanPeet)

Woolsey Beauregard Jackson
Stokeley settled in Mink's Prairie
with his wife Annice. They bought
their fifty acres for six bales of cotton.
Later, fifty six more were bought for
$280. Lester, Leila, and Edna were
three of their ten children.
(Courtesy of Celeste Graves)

Of course, no review of colorful place names in the county could be complete without mentioning our own Cut'N Shoot. Variants of its source abound but one fairly reliable version traces the name to an incident in July, 1912. The residents had built a Community House as an interdenominational meeting place with the specific exclusion of Mormons and Apostolics. That month, a popular preacher came to town to preach but he was said by some to be apostolic. His use of the Hall split the town, leading to an open, armed confrontation on July 20. A young boy in the crowd was overheard to say, "I'm scared. I'm going to cut around the corner and shoot through those bushes." Fortunately no lives were lost. Preacher Stamps stayed all summer but held his meetings outdoors. Town leaders, though, became so fond of the tale that the designation stuck.

T. J. Goodson was born (1858) in Goodson Prairie. In 1892, he and his wife Winnie were the first home builders in the new Mink's Prairie town on the IG&N railroad. Tom farmed and worked in a sawmill. Later, when the town became Magnolia, he opened a cordwood business using the railroad to expand his dream. Our early citizens, like the county itself, were always ready to grow and build on new opportunities. (Courtesy of Celeste Graves)

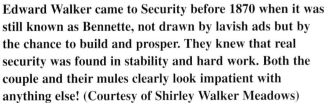

Edward Walker came to Security before 1870 when it was still known as Bennette, not drawn by lavish ads but by the chance to build and prosper. They knew that real security was found in stability and hard work. Both the couple and their mules clearly look impatient with anything else! (Courtesy of Shirley Walker Meadows)

The Isaac Conroe home typically boasts a porch, a swing, chairs, plants and children—the future of the county. Mrs. William Conroe on the porch watches them, especially Lois (on the left.) She was later to become Lois Wooldridge. This house on the corner of A and First Street was later used as a temporary courthouse. (Courtesy of Edmona Wooldridge Bowden)

Lands, titles, and names of towns are all part of our history, but the families that settled and prospered here truly incorporate the dream of our county. The early settlers understood that a vision can only become a verity if it is reborn in the future. They affirmed their belief in this future for they created these homes to hold families, planned their community, plowed and planted the land, to enable their children to build on the foundations of their dream.

The Carson home in Willis was built by A. M. Carson, a tobacco and cotton farmer who was also co–owner of the Carson–Morris Store. The road in front later became old Highway 75. Note the windmill and the telephone wire side by side. Technology was here at last! (Courtesy of Caroline Cryar)

In 1911 Roy Dean built this home for his family in Magnolia—for $700! His father, William Dean, had settled in Mink's Prairie in 1871. Roy and his brothers ran a general store along with working cattle, land and timber. (Courtesy of Celeste Graves)

In 1885, Robert and Florentine Damuth bought one hundred acres at Tillis Prairie, near Magnolia. Their son, John, was born in 1887 and married Belle in 1908. This is their wedding portrait. John carried on the dream: first as a farmer and carpenter, then an oil field worker and finally a building engineer for the courthouse. (Courtesy of Celeste Graves)

Luella and Charles Pinkney Gayle and family were residents of Magnolia. His father had earlier lived in Danville, but like so many others left there around 1889. (Courtesy of Celeste Graves)

William Butler, Sr., came here from Virginia probably as a slave of the Clepper family. At Lem Clepper's death, Sophie, Butler's widow was given one hundred acres. This land known as Butler's Crossing is at the intersection of FM1488 and FM149. This picture shows some of their descendants in 1926.
(Courtesy of Celeste Graves)

Turn of the century Conroe was "uptown" in spite of its unpaved streets. The fancy building on the corner was the bank. Ladies' millinery could be purchased right beside it. This scene is taken at the corner of Simonton and Avenue Two, now Pacific.
(Courtesy of Caroline Cryar)

Birdie Bennett (third from the left) lived at Butler's Crossing and walked everyday to Magnolia where she worked as a domestic for many families. In addition, she was active in her church and in the PTA. Her mother had been a slave, but Birdie was very much a part of the dream of this county. (Courtesy of Celeste Graves)

Albert Wade King and his wife Era are proud of their new home on South First in Conroe. Their first house had a dirt floor which Era swept clean every day. Albert was born in Danville but moved to Conroe and was a school custodian. Here they raised five children and at least one dog! (Courtesy of Dortha Altman)

As towns grew, many had first lived in frame built "town" homes such as that of Sam and Ethel Godsey near the Santa Fe Railroad on what is now South Frazier in Conroe. (Courtesy of Shirley Walker Meadows)

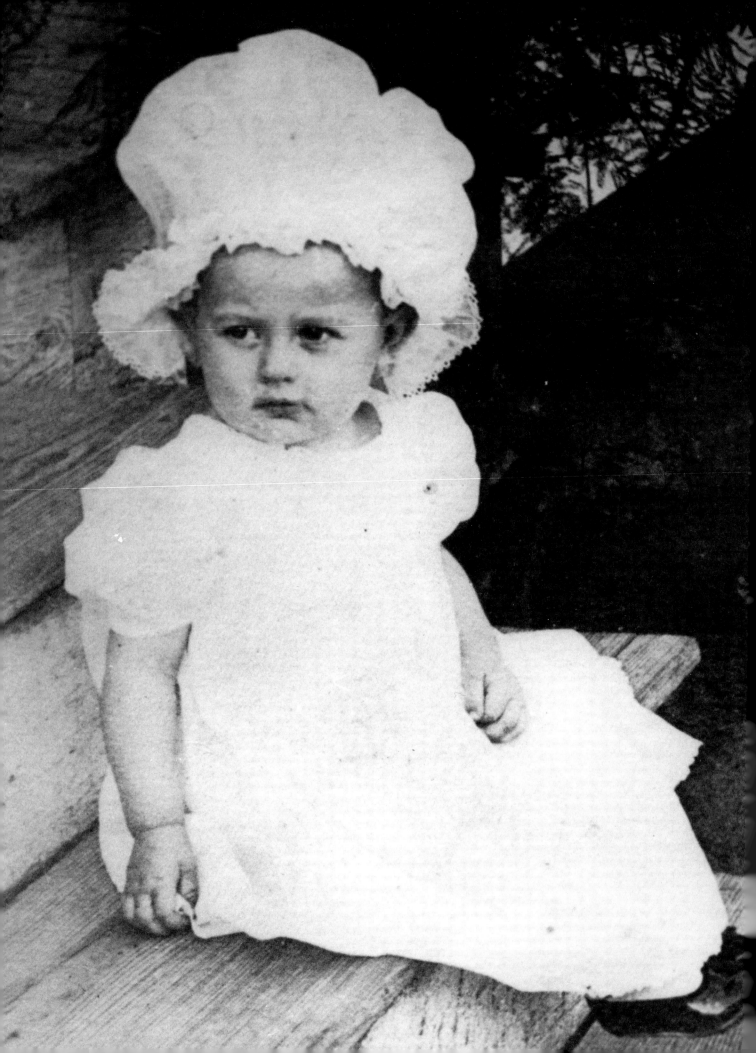

Because the dream of Montgomery
County was given these dimensions, it
became a thing of permanence, a home
for many people to settle and grow in.
Consider these four pictures of Mrs.
Annie Harrell: a child, a young
woman, a gracious lady, and a pillar of
her community in her golden years.
Her story, repeated over and over, is
the story of Montgomery County.
(Courtesy of Dolores Harrell)

Building on the Foundations of the Dream

As Montgomery County grew and prospered, the resourcefulness and independence of our early settlers met the need to inter-relate. Isolated farms needed transportation, communication, supplies, and public services in order to survive.

Of course, some transportation already existed; they all arrived here somehow. Most had come in carts and wagons drawn by oxen or draft horses. These vehicles supplied vital farming uses as well but were slow due to the lack of adequate roads. It took an oxcart as much as four to five days to make the trip into Houston with a load of crops and to return. Stagecoaches provided means of travel for some, taking into consideration that Montgomery was located on the main stage line from Houston to Huntsville as well as from Washington on the Brazos. Visitors who were staying the night might seek the services of Price's Hotel where a bell in the yard summoned them to dinner each evening. In Conroe, they might enjoy Madeley's Hotel next to the railroad, or choose the Chrisman Hotel (at present-day

Teams such as these took loads of cotton or lumber to Houston and brought back needed supplies. This scene in Magnolia around 1920 shows the growth of transportation, communication and business systems so vital to the county's growth. (Courtesy of Celeste Graves)

Collins and Pacific) where in the late 1800s a patron could have all he could eat for only $1! The railroads, too, brought an influx of travelers as well as being a major source of income for many county residents.

Finally automobiles arrived. Mr. Joe Chrisman had the first auto in the county while Dr. W. P. Ingrum had the 32nd. He was so proud of this that he had the number thirty two painted on all his subsequent cars! In 1910 the towns of Montgomery, Willis, Magnolia, and Security were a day's drive away but in 1923, according to a Conroe Courier Almanac 'the average traveler can get there by breakfast.' People were on the move in Montgomery County.

Oxen were sturdy animals able to pull plows, cultivators, and wagons. The owner, C. E. Johnson, reports they took four days to yoke break but then were so gentle his son could ride them. He had lived in several Texas towns but tells us, "Once I tasted the well water from Montgomery County, I would always stay there." (Courtesy of Celeste Graves)

No working cart this! In 1901 Ike Walker of Security was probably all set up to go "a-courting" in this horse and carriage. (Courtesy of Shirley Walker Meadows)

A typical wagon and oxen team, c. 1915 in Magnolia. Mr. Springer, the owner, stands on the wagon while Estelle Gayle and Lester Goodson look on. Wagons were the mainstay of early transportation. (Courtesy of Celeste Graves)

The old Montgomery–Willis Road bridge saw many a wagon cross. It's now deep under Lake Conroe. (Courtesy of Markey Heintz)

Every farmer had or wanted a horse. Jack Robinson of New Caney looks very much at home on his in 1915. No Rhinestone Cowboys around here!

Road workers made travel much better for residents. Sam Godsey (far right) worked at this trade as well as construction and farming. Road crews are still frequent sights around the county although their equipment is heavier! (Courtesy of Shirley Walker Meadows)

Of course, transportation included the building of roads and bridges. Jack King remembers making the trip to Houston by wagon to bring back flour and sugar to Danville stores and eating prairie chickens on the way. Bridges such as this made a big difference and took advantage of the latest technology such as these two metal smokestacks which the crews called "donkies." (Courtesy of Dortha Altman)

Even the children had to get around! Proud parents Clara and Richard Knight must have enjoyed showing off their daughter Ercelle in her stylish stroller. Quite a contrast to the plexiglass and padding of today's models.

Here at the old Price Hotel in Montgomery, stagecoach travelers could find a comfortable stop. Most were farmers or lumber businessmen but General Sam Houston often stopped here as well. The hotel was built in the early 1840s and later known as the Rabon and then the Berkley Hotel.

When children outgrew strollers but were not old enough to drive, parents had to get innovative. Betty Stinson had a truly unique goat cart. (Courtesy of Betty S. Gowing)

A typical hotel of the early days (1890–1900), this one in Conroe offered a location close to the railroad but near downtown businesses. (The courthouse can be seen in the background.) Perhaps Caroline Cryar can tell you about rates and services because that is her great-grandmother, Sarah Frances Frolick, on the porch. (Courtesy of Caroline Cryar)

The Wooldridge Hotel in Willis was built in the 1870s again primarily to serve railroad traffic. In 1872 for example, 91,600 immigrants came to Texas, most by rail with all their possessions in box cars. Those whose destination was Montgomery County, like the Pratts of Willis, found a place to stay until they could purchase land or find housing. (Courtesy of John Massey)

The Conroe Hotel (later the Chrisman and then the McGee) was built in 1908 right beside the railroad track to serve passengers. Even after rail traffic diminished, Mrs. McGee served wonderful home cooked meals family style. Her hotel was also home to her two sons and several homeless boys who, because of her, were able to finish high school and to take part in its sports program.

The King Hotel, later the Pursley, was a large railroad hotel in Willis. (Courtesy of Jesse Traylor)

No old shoes or cans, no painted messages—but bride and groom Mildred and Clint Gayle pose with their wedding party on May 5, 1917, in Conroe. Reverend and Mrs. Ellis are seen inside the yard. (Courtesy of Celeste Graves)

W. A. Dean demonstrates that running those Model T's in 1921 took work! But hard work was a family legacy. His father, W. A. Dean, Sr., came here in 1849, married Margaret Shannon and later, as a widower, Cora Campbell. All loved him, calling him "Uncle Billie." He farmed, was the local mail carrier on horseback, and worked as a carpenter. (Courtesy of Celeste Graves)

By 1939 the Texas Highway Department had an office in Conroe and even offered a first–aid team. (Courtesy of Dortha Altman)

In the 1930s better roads, oil, and building booms enabled many families to own a "family" car such as Ethel and Sam Godsey. Daughter Lorene and nephew Clifford look eager to go. In the 1930s a trip to Dallas was a major all day trek with maybe a stop for a bite to eat at the old Buffalo Bus Depot about halfway there. (Courtesy of Shirley Walker Meadows)

Those who came to Conroe or left it by bus during the early forties will remember the Trailways station on the corner of Main and Davis at Carter's Drug Store. Robin and Hattie Stinson Carter might have welcomed them.

M. P. Daniel was at one time the publisher of the *Willis Progress*. Later he married and moved to Dayton where he became the father of Price Daniel, a state governor, and Bill Daniel, once the U. S. Governor of Guam. (Courtesy of Doris Daniel)

But news had to travel too! Soon we began to develop communication systems. The trading posts were the first hub of civic interchange as they afforded a gathering place for the local residents. Mail came by stagecoach once a week from Houston and by horseback from Washington on the Brazos. In 1854 the first telegraph lines went up with the wires following the old pioneer trail from Montgomery to Houston and Huntsville. The route became known as "Telegraph Road." Before 1900 there was one telephone line to Gilbert's Drug Store. The publication of our first newspaper began on April 26, 1845. Its publisher, John M. Wade, had come here in the 1830's, served as deputy surveyor, and fought at San Jacinto. Fittingly, he called his paper *The Montgomery Patriot*. Subscribers paid only $4 for fifty two issues— a real bargain. Unfortunately, Wade closed down after only one year. Later, Montgomery had *The Register* (1870), Willis, *The Observer* (1889) and *The Progress* (1908), and in Conroe Mr. Jones established *The Courier* in 1892. The *Conroe Enterprise* (1893) later merged with *The Courier*. O. Etheridge began a career as editor of *The Courier* in 1911. We were now linked to one another and to the larger world through different communication systems.

In 1909 there was no such thing as a Central Post Office or home delivery of mail. Here a group of Montgomery men wait on the porch of Dr. J. L. Irons' office for the daily delivery.

Leland B. Everett II (1893–1976) was an early owner, editor, and publisher of the *Conroe Courier* as well as a businessman involved in Everett and Sons Hardware and Grocery stores. (Courtesy of Mrs. Anne Moore)

By World War II communications had come a long way. This scene at the Conroe Telephone Company (in the Madeley Building next to Talley's Domino Hall on Simonton) reminds us of the days when an actual person asked "Number please?" and we responded with a three-digit-number. (Courtesy of Vera Acrey)

Dr. James M. Ware and his wife Lelia on their wedding day in 1905 were valued citizens of Magnolia. He made house calls, first on horseback, then by buggy and finally by automobile. (Courtesy of Celeste Graves)

Left: Lois Williams was the wife of one of Conroe's early postmasters, Gary Williams. Her daughter Suzanne, now Suzie Brignac, models the Shirley Temple curls so much a "must" for young girls around 1940. Lois Griffin's family were original settlers (1828) and her father B. D. Griffin served as County Clerk in 1884. (Courtesy of Suzie Williams Brignac)

Right: Sheriff E. T. "Hoss" Anderson learned the tradition of law and order from his father who was sheriff from 1902–1920. The elder Anderson was a "farmer and a gentleman," typical of our early citizens who settled, farmed, worked and still found time to serve the community—often for no pay.

With growth came the need for public services. Earlier, county residents relied on home remedies and most illnesses were treated at home or the area doctor came to the home. Yes, they made house calls! In larger towns, doctors might see patients in an office located in their own home. In 1874 the Medical Register listed 12 doctors in the county and in 1904 doctors who belonged to the Medical Association paid state dues of $2 and county dues of $1. A good picture of such early practitioners is Dr. T. S. Falvey. He was the Foster Lumber Company doctor and Conroe's first major surgeon. He made house calls in a Model-T (or a buggy if the roads were too muddy) and often operated on a kitchen table assisted by his nurse, Miss Laura Thompson. Eventually, he had offices in downtown Montgomery.

The Mary Swain Sanitarium on Davis and Third in Conroe was built by Dr. T. S. Falvey to honor his mother. (Courtesy of Shirley Walker Meadows)

Dr. Powell graduated from Tulane, came to Galveston by ship and walked to Waverley to become a county resident. Later, he lived and practiced in Willis. He often invited patients to stay in his thirteen room home where the cook–stoves were always lighted at 4:30 a.m. to cook for as many as twenty people daily. (Courtesy of Jesse Traylor)

New businesses often built up near the railroad but the general stores were the earliest. But soon residents could find drug stores such as Carter's Drug in Conroe in 1892 or Collier Drug on Pacific where Sam Hailey went to work in 1898. One year later he opened his own Capitol Drug Store. Citizens could shop at furniture stores, dry good stores, livery stables, and blacksmith shops. Cotton gins enabled local farmers to process their crops. Dr. J. H. Price built the first gin in the early 1840s, nine miles SW of Montgomery and George Dean had a horse-powered gin on Ford's Lake. By 1866 New Caney even boasted a steam-powered gin. The Copeland Gin operated from 1880 to 1890 and a large gin was run by the Weisingers where April Sound is now located. (After 1920, gin activity declined and many closed.)

Public services improved as well. Road crews made transportation easier while the civic buildings enhanced life. For example, when Samuel W. Godsey arrived here in 1904, he found extensive construction work in addition to his farming. He worked on many of the sidewalks in downtown Conroe always using a hand-carved wooded stamp to sign all of his cement work. Prosperity brought banks, too. In Conroe, a bank was chartered as early as 1906 and First State Bank opened in 1912. First National Bank, the oldest still operating bank opened in 1914. To regulate such vitality and growth, we needed "law and order." Earlier, much governing and policing had been done

With all those horse-drawn vehicles and riding horses, blacksmithing was an important business. While many farmers did their own such work, shops did exist like Bert Sander's place in Montgomery, 1900–1920. Perhaps Bert should have bartered with a roofer!

Another large gin near Montgomery with some of its product—cotton bales stacked in front.

Cotton gins such as this one also appeared. This one first owned by a Mr. Fields was later operated by Russell Berkley in Montgomery.

by the citizens who saw such service as their civic duty. But now they found a need for more formalized services—courts, county offices, and law enforcement. Fire Departments were a welcome addition. The Conroe Fire Department in 1918 had only two pieces of equipment, hand-drawn hose reels which were occasionally hitched to a Model-T Ford. The first fire station was built in 1923—too late to fight the devastating fires in Conroe in 1901 and 1911. In the latter blaze Conroe's twenty-five downtown buildings were reduced to only three!

The Conroe Ice Co. was run by "Sima" Stillings for thirty years (1927–1956). The first plant was on S. Main and this new one on E. Davis in Conroe. (Courtesy of Harold Stillings)

Here cotton bales wait to be shipped at the Magnolia depot. Such businesses and the developing railroad gave residents market opportunities. The bales gave the station agent a chance for a bit of R and R. (Courtesy of Celeste Graves)

In Magnolia, young "Hig" Yon worked at Stockley's General Store and later purchased it. When he heard that the Railroad was coming through in 1920, he opened a new store and operated it until 1957. Notice it was also the local post office! (Courtesy of Celeste Graves)

The Carson–Morris Store was one of our earliest serving Willis even before 1900. (Courtesy of Caroline Cryar)

The Willis Mercantile is open with the owner Melville Paddock and clerk "Scraps" Powell ready to sell their goods like those suspenders on the front rack. (Courtesy of Jesse Traylor)

Alfred Marion Carson kept an office in Willis as well as the general store and a tobacco and cotton farm. The safe protected his profits and the bookkeeping table allowed careful records to be kept. The invoice shown is careful, indeed, as his clerk J. M. Golding had even recorded a fifty cent overcharge on a meal. (a. Caroline Cryar, b. Russ Clanton)

Russ Clanton worked at the Thomason Store on Danville Road in Willis for $30 a month plus room and board. As a fringe benefit he could use his boss' car on dates. (Courtesy of Russ Clanton)

Max Rothenberg left Lithuania at age 11, arriving in New York and gaining his citizenship in 1919. When he and his wife Lillian first came to Conroe, he worked at Holland and Andur Furniture. In 1932, he bought out the business and opened his own store on Main near the Crighton Theater later moving to Simonton Street (Courtesy of Dianna Dushkin)

But clearly Montgomery County was building on the foundations of the dream. One family's story reflects this growth. The S. W. Godsey's came here by train in 1904 but brought two draft-horses. They farmed, raised their children, and he did construction work. In 1910 Mrs. Godsey's father, William L. Keller, while riding a wagon across the Santa Fe track's rough crossing, was killed when his rifle discharged. In 1920 the Godsey's returned to the county by automobile after a brief stay in Oklahoma but he still carried a Winchester on the trip for safety. During the 1930s electricity arrived. Mr. Godsey, in the spirit of high technology, modified a truck by adding curtains and seats. The truck was then used as a school bus and a "recreational vehicle" for summer camping.

John Wahrenberger quickly saw the needs of this growing area, and his store on the corner of Davis and Main in Conroe met many of those needs. Wonder if that mule is looking for millinery? The large store, redone in brick after 1911, became one of the first department stores in Texas, offering everything from dry goods to furniture, ready-to-wear clothes and fabrics. (Courtesy of Caroline Cryar)

Sadly, in 1932, he approached the railroad track where a tank car was being filled with gas. The gas had over-flowed, its fumes stalled his car, and restarting it ignited the gas. Both he and his seventeen year old son were badly burned but recovered and received a $10,000 cash settlement from the railroad lawyers. What did they do with the money? Not at all disenchanted by their family troubles with roads, wagons, and railroads, the Godsey's bought two new cars. (One tan with orange wheels and the other black with red wheels.) Yes, life was now a far cry from the plodding oxcarts of one hundred years earlier!

D. P. McFarland's store on the southeast corner of Simonton and Thompson in Conroe with its owners Mallie and Drew and their children Maidel, Jamie, and Drew, Jr. Everybody worked in the store. Drew, Sr., was an ordained minister as well, preaching at Honea, Security, and Montgomery. (Courtesy of Gertie Spencer)

Everett's Cash Grocery succeeded certainly in part due to its owner's understanding of his patrons. He stayed open every night until the last Santa Fe train brought customers from the sawmills. Then, and only then, he rang this closing bell and walked home carrying the strongbox under his arm with a lantern in the other hand. Here Mark Wilmot Everett, Jr., carries on the tradition. (Courtesy of Meta Stephens)

Henry Bascom Everett and his wife Iola came here after the Civil War, first to Houston and then to Conroe where he was Depot Agent. He quickly saw a need for a business and opened Everett's Cash Grocery in 1908. The family then included Mark and Mary Everett, H. Bascom Will (standing) and Carl, H. B. Jr., Lucy, Little Iola, Iola with her first grandchild Wilmot, and Leland. (Courtesy of Anne Moore)

The local drug store became a hub as the trading post had been earlier—not because we were a drug culture but because these businesses offered a variety of services. Here Dr. F. A. Younger stands in front of Peynghous Drug Store in Montgomery in 1910. The telephone office was located upstairs.

Expansion in the 1930s brought new public services among them the first public sewerage! Here we see pipes being put into place in the one thousand block of Roberson in Conroe. How much we take for granted these days! (Courtesy of Billie Lynch)

Business, at least in Conroe, was dealt a blow in 1911 when a fire wiped out most of the downtown buildings. This one, the Conroe First National Bank at Main and Davis, was one of the few to survive and is today a law office.

Many of us remember the interior of Capital Drug Store on Main Street in Conroe. Here, Sam Hailey, Sr., Myron Colemen, and Sam, Jr. (left to right) would fill our prescriptions, sell us notions, or fix us a malt. There was even curb service! (Courtesy of Martha Welschans)

During World War II when men were not available for such work, women took their place. Not willing to totally retreat after the war, they formed a Women's Auxiliary.

Our Volunteer Firemen were an active unit in the community, Here, they are collecting toys for needy children at Christmas. Their equipment may not have been state-of-the-art but their civic dedication certainly was!

Nathaniel Hart Davis arrived in Montgomery on April 4, 1840, to practice law. But he did much more than that. He served the Republic in the Somerville Expedition, was a dedicated public servant, Mayor of Montgomery, Circuit Judge, and Justice of the Peace. His legal work set many precedents. Much of this civic work went unpaid, a contribution to the county. Many of our early leaders accepted such posts, receiving no reward but their pride in the growth of the county. (Courtesy of Martha and Harley Gandy)

Justice John Sullivan of New Caney served as judge around 1900 and added much to our growing government systems. (Courtesy of John Armour)

Judge William McGuffin Williams (1864–1951) was born in Seguin, Texas but came to Conroe in 1903. Here he played an active part in law and order. A member of the Texas and the Montgomery County Bar Association, he worked as a lawyer with his brother-in-law W. N. Foster and served as County Attorney from 1912–1918. (Courtesy of Suzanne Williams Brignac)

Grover Cleveland Mostyn (center), born at Tillis Prairie near Magnolia, farmed and raised cattle on the Mostyn Ranch. During the Depression he became County Commissioner to supplement his income and when the family home burned, he worked as deputy sheriff for Guy Hooper. Later, Grover was Sheriff for six years. (Courtesy of Celeste Graves)

Another public servant of note was Edwin A. Stephan. Eddie was appointed by
Mayor Crighton in 1935 as "a one-man police force." Known to all the young people,
he kept watch over a town where we could walk anywhere and feel safe. He even
kept tabs on the high school "courters" at the band hall in the evenings! The habit of
uniforms came early it seems for here his Aunt Frieda has him dressed in a Buster
Brown suit posing with a replica of the famous Tige. (Courtesy of Meta Stephan)

The original county courthouse in Montgomery was a log cabin built in 1838. In 1842 it was replaced with a two-story frame building. Funds for this first courthouse and a jail were provided from sixty acres of land donated by William Sheppard.

Conroe became the county seat in 1889 and in 1891 built a courthouse and a jail of red bricks manufactured right here. The property, deeded to the county by J. K. Ayres for $1, was on the block where the old Nations Bank and the old Library sat. (Courtesy of Anne Moore)

In 1936 tax revenues from the oil fields made it possible to complete the present courthouse. Since its completion on November 4, 1936, extensive changes have been made but the site and basic design are still the same. (Courtesy of Vera Acrey)

In this building, the workings of the county go on every working day. This scene taken in 1940, catches Virgil Cochran, Tax Assessor c. 1940 (center). Beside him in glasses is Joe B. Stinson and second from the right is young Whitson Etheridge. (Courtesy of Betty Stinson Gowing)

In 1909 the courthouse was plastered on the outside. Sam Godsey was with the construction crew for this job. (Courtesy of Shirley Walker Meadows)

Making the Dream Work

Those who came here were not drawn by the promise of jobs but of land. Very few industries developed. There was a pottery factory on Juggery Creek, mostly for the local production of whiskey jugs, bowls, and churns. In 1843 A. Martin opened a tannery which operated until the Civil War. The only truly thriving industry was from the tobacco grown here. In 1895 Willis had eight tobacco factories shipping all over the United States. When the Spanish-American War cut off the supply of Cuban cigars in 1891, sales boomed but when the tariff was lifted, the industry dried up. Montgomery County's economy clearly had four mainstays in its development: farming, timber, railroads, and oil.

Farming of course, was the primary livelihood of the early settlers. They had come for land and many had been farmers before arriving in Texas. They planted cotton for cash, corn for feed, peas, sweet potatoes, melons, sugar cane, and peanuts for their own sustenance. The typical farm house was built of wood with a long porch across the front, fireplaces on either end, and rarely painted. Around it would be a well, an "outhouse," perhaps a spring house,

Rich farm lands drew hardworking families whose efforts yielded the growth not only of crops but of the dream for many generations. (Courtesy of Markey Heintz)

a forge, a syrup mill, and a barn. Because there were no screens, net "mosquito bars" or smoking coals were relied on to deter mosquitoes and strips of fly paper hung in each of the rooms.

The men spent their days tending the crops or taking care of the livestock. While cattle raising never reached the proportions of the Western areas, many farms had milk cows, hogs, chickens, and maybe goats. Honey bees were cultivated and five hundred eighty seven hives were recorded in 1920. Each season of the year brought its own set of chores. For example, after harvest, sweet potatoes were stored in "dry mounds." A shallow pit was dug, lined with palmettos and pinestraw, and filled with potatoes. These pits were then covered and provided food throughout the year. When the first freeze came, it was time to butcher hogs—a big operation. The hog was killed (shot or hit in the head), bled, scalded, hung for scraping, and then butchered. Many times neighbors came to help with cutting the hams and bacon, stuffing sausage, etc.

Inside the farmhouses the women were just as busy. They did all the washing and boiling of clothes in big cast-iron pots using home-made lye soap. Then they ironed with flat-irons heated in the kerosene stove or fireplace. Their clothes were often homemade with calico and percale material being sold for five to ten cents a yard. The kitchen was never idle as canning or churning were regular activities. Often, extra eggs were gathered and sold (twenty cents a dozen) or buttermilk was sold for ten cents per gallon. When they did get a minute for a cup of coffee, they first had to parch it for the coffee was sold green.

Such forefathers and foremothers were of hardy stock. They overcame hardship and loss while pursuing their dream. Henry Jones and his wife Ann came here from Dothan, Alabama by ship to Galveston then by train to Willis around 1868. Henry, legally blind, nevertheless farmed and raised cattle, chicken, and hogs. Consider Edward Watter who came here from Louisiana after his first wife died at the birth of their son Wesley. Edward bore up, raised the baby, remarried in 1879 and homesteaded one hundred sixty acres in the Security area.

Not only industry but vision abounded. That ability to see a solution, to turn a problem into growth was epitomized in John Michael Weisinger, born in Danville in 1868. He met his wife Mary Etta of Bear Bend and on Christmas Day in 1892 they began their life together in Ryals (what is April Sound today). Together they farmed four thousand acres using the labor of twenty three tenant farmers, most of them black. To meet the demands of such a "spread," Weisinger added a gristmill, a gin, a carriage house, a general store, a syrup mill, a blacksmith shop, barns, and at a later date even a private water system and an electric plant. When the land needed clearing, he had the

Tobacco, an early cash crop, was grown on large plantations. After harvest leaves were cured in barns. They were processed at one of seven cigar factories in Willis like this one founded by Capt. T. W. Smith after the Civil War. From the factory, cigars were shipped in distinctive boxes all over the United States.

Not all were fortunate enough to own land yet they worked it for others as sharecroppers like Suzy and Leonard Blair of Montgomery. Later, this couple became caretakers not of land but of Mr. McComb at his lake home. (Courtesy of Wanda Jordan)

"wild" idea of bringing in fifty goats. That worked so well that eventually there were six hundred and enough land was kept arable. When the popular long staple cotton proved not as productive as the short staple variety, he renovated his gin so that it could handle the better variety.

Mary Etta's discipline was no less creative. All eleven of the children worked. If the boys were caught "lollygagging" they had to sweep the front porch wearing a bonnet and a skirt! Mary cleaned her floors with lye soap, cooked, quilted, and found time to serve as Worthy Matron of Eastern Star. Her husband was Superintendent of the Sunday School for the Montgomery Methodist Church also being active in the Masonic Order.

Because of this energy, vision, and determination the farms grew and flourished. By 1920, the population was around 20,000 and 80,605 acres were under cultivation. One record lists 1,029 farms, itemizing their owners as "783—White, 223— Colored, and 23— foreign born White." Dairy products netted $38,413; chickens and eggs, $22,452. Over 15,000 acres of corn and cotton were harvested in the year 1920.

And yet, one columnist warned "As timber is cut, lands decrease in value. We need to enlarge agriculture because revenues cannot be raised any other way." How wrong he was! Montgomery County had many resources and adaptable residents to make those resources profitable. Early settlers had been drawn by the dream of farm land, but they soon found thick forests as well. It was from these Piney Woods that the county's next economic thrust was to come.

Henry and Priscilla Mostyn, who arrived here in 1849 to farm near Tillis Prairie were typical of our early settlers. They established a productive farm and when he died, she kept it going, adding to their holdings and rearing six children. This picture shows their place between Magnolia and Montgomery in 1896. (Courtesy of Celeste Graves)

Sugar cane mills were another early business since ribbon cane syrup was the most popular sweetener. Here, Bill Fritch of Magnolia is loading his wagon with cane to take to the Sugar Cane Mill on Lake Creek between Magnolia and Montgomery around 1920. (Courtesy of Celeste Graves)

Another small business serving farmers was the dairy. At the Calfee Dairy one hundred cows had to be milked twice a day—by hand! Unfortunately this required beginning at 2 a.m. (Courtesy of Gary Calfee)

Although razorbacks such as these were not exactly domesticated, farmers and the local Indians depended on them for food, The farmers took time to hunt when they needed pork, bacon, or ham.

Of course almost every farm had chickens! Here, Lee and Missouri Needham tend theirs. Their homestead was on what is now Needham Road South of Conroe. Lee also found time to serve on the school board.
(Courtesy of Barbara Bishop)

The S. W. Godsey family bought sixty two acres on the Schaefer Road (now Crighton Cutoff near Conroe) around 1915. They built this log barn where they lived until they could afford a larger house. In this barn they weathered the hurricane of 1915! Five years later the better house was done. Their well used a small diameter bucket with a shutter bottom, which opened when the bucket hit water and closed when it was pulled up full. The large tank behind the house caught rainwater. This spread was behind what is now River Plantation. (Courtesy of Shirley Walker Meadows)

Crops were often grown to feed the family but work did not end when the harvest was done. Sweet potatoes had to be stored in "dry mounds"— pits lined with palmettos and pine straw from which the delicious vegetables could be taken all winter long. (Courtesy of Shirley Walker Meadows)

Farming meant almost constant work. The forest and the fields had to be cleared and fire wood had to be supplied. Employees of Homer Calfee, Alex Williams and a co-worker are taking care of chores such as those around 1930. (Courtesy of Gary Calfee)

Hay had to be grown to feed the livestock. At first, farmers had to hand-load the crop on wagons with the help of the entire family. (Courtesy of Celeste Graves)

Plowing was also a long but essential activity. Homer Calfee stops long enough to enjoy the cool drink his wife Delphia brought to him after walking through the field. Today that field would be on Longmire Road. (Courtesy of Gary Calfee)

At home work still continued. Homer and Delphia are cooking muscadine grapes for jelly. (Courtesy of Gary Calfee)

Here Delphia cleans a batch of catfish for a fish fry later. Charlie Peters helps as young Dick and Lula Belle Calfee look on.
(Courtesy of Gary Calfee)

The fruit of all this work was a bounteous table. Often it was laid "on the grounds", not because they loved the outdoors, but because everyone simply could not fit in those small houses. (Courtesy of Gary Calfee)

Children had chores and learned to be self-sufficient. Dick and Lula Belle could fetch the water while churning was sometimes turned over to the older children (Courtesy of Gary Calfee)

It was quite a relief to the farmers (and to the mules) when modernization brought trucks like this for the hauling of hay and supplies such as these big sacks of grain. (Courtesy of Celeste Graves)

"Papa" Jim Simonton plowed with his favorite mule. His family had quite a tradition about mules. Reuben Davis Simonton refused to surrender after Appomatox, instead riding his mule "Ike" all the way from South Carolina to here. He even rode Ike while serving as our first Democratic Sheriff after reconstruction and buried him in the front lawn of the Marvin Simonton home in Montgomery (Courtesy of Katy Dean Hill)

To keep cattle free of insects ranchers ran them through dipping vats like Sanders Vat S. of Magnolia on FM 1774. (Courtesy of Celeste Graves)

Cattle did supply some income. Here Bill Brantley of Magnolia is busy branding his herd. He recalls early times when he made the four day round trip to Houston, staying overnight at Henke's Wagon Yard. Perhaps it was those experiences which led him to run a freight company later in which his wife Bertie did most of the driving. (Courtesy of Celeste Graves)

Cattle took priority over other traffic when a drive was in progress. Here a herd goes right through downtown Magnolia where the town water tank afforded them a drink. (Courtesy of Celeste Graves)

MILLS

Although farming never stopped, by the early 1900s more of the county's economic base began to rest not in its soil but in its saw mills. Earlier small mills called "pecker-wood" mills had existed to serve local needs while George Dean had a large mill seven miles South of Montgomery in the 1860s. But it was because of the railroads that timber was a viable industry here. Wood products from Montgomery County were soon being shipped nationwide. First, the mills processed virgin timber creating lumber, cross-ties, and cordwood. Later they found markets of second and third growth timber when pulpwood came into demand around 1930.

In its heyday, logging brought in around $3 million annually and supplied the major livelihood for 3,000–4,000 workers. A few of the major mills were those of Isaac Conroe at Beech, the Cowl Spur Mill near Conroe, the Hunt Lumber Company at Willis, the Keystone Mill at Waukegan, the Foster Lumber Company at Fostoria, and the Grogan-Cochran Lumber Company near Tamina. The Delta Land and Timber Company, established in 1914, brought in "state-of-the-art" equipment and techniques.

Whether large or small, these mills followed essentially the same procedure. Timber had to be cut and the large logs brought to the mill for further work. At first this transport was done by wagons, drawn by oxen,

Here log wagons, usually pulled by eight oxen, bring a load of logs to the Nichols Sawmill in Magnolia, c. 1920. The owners often brought these wagons with them when they came carrying all their possessions with them. At the mills, logs were dried and planed before shipping.

mules, or horses with only eight to ten logs being carried at one time. Later, some mills were able to use rails for the job. At the Foster Mill, workers were transported to the forests on a small train called "Old Smokey" and a log train called "Dinky" brought the logs back to the mill. The logs were then dried in wood-burning kilns about twenty four square feet in area and sixteen feet high with 2x12 joists half way up to hold the logs. When the kiln was full of green lumber, the kiln was fired (smoked). Later, the dried wood was processed at the planing mill before being loaded onto trains for shipping. All of these areas were connected by dolly-ways thirteen feet wide and four feet off the ground. The actual dollies ran on two wheels with two men to work on each dolly.

Obviously this complex operation required many laborers. The companies ensured their labor-supply by creating towns, mill towns, and complete communities. The typical mill town had a large company store or commissary, quarters for the workers and their families, and a company doctor. At the Waukegan mill the owner lived in the "Big House" and perhaps a few managers had large houses as well but workers had either a boarding

This scene at a sawmill near Montgomery shows those indispensable oxen waiting for a load. Later larger mills had access to tram lines and the oxen were not so vital to the process anymore. (Courtesy of Anna Davis Weisinger)

At the mill, logs were first cut into "cants", square poles created by cutting off the round outer sections. Then cants were sent to the planer mill where they were cut into various lengths of lumber. This planer mill crew is working at Waukegan, c. 1915.

This crew waits on the platform for the next tram of logs. Most of them lived at the mill, either in a boarding house or in a millhouse with their family. They not only worked at the mill but played and worshipped there as well. Clubs and churches were provided carefully segregated on one side of the track or the other.

house or lived in small four-room houses built of 1x12 batt and board. White workers lived on the north side of the tracks while black workers found quarters on the south. Such segregation was everywhere; separate churches, clubs, etc. existed on each side of the track. The boarding house at Grogan's Mill had thirty-two rooms, two men per room. The houses rented for $3–8 per month. This rent was withheld from the paycheck on the last Thursday of each month as was a $1 fee for water. All other utilities were free. Medical services sometimes had a fee also.

The workers received anywhere from $1 to $2.50 per day and there were no set hours. A typical schedule was six days a week, ten hours a day. This pay was given in company coinage which was accepted at the company store and many local stores. If necessary, a worker could convert these tokens to cash at the company office. Only three holidays a year were granted: July 4, Christmas Day, and June 19 (Emancipation Day) (also called Juneteenth). On Juneteenth no black man had to work and some companies threw a big barbecue for their black employees.

Keystone Mill at Waukegan like other mills kept logs in ponds to deter insect damage. Behind the pond are workers' houses provided by the owners at minimal rent, sometimes free.

The pictures below will show you that the logging life was not an easy one for the men, women, or children, but it did provide income for many families. Even during the Depression these mills continued to operate. (The Foster Mill shut down in 1957 and the Cochran Mill in 1960). Along with the railroads, the timber industry constituted the largest payroll in the county for over forty years.

Workers at the Pitts Mill in Keenan around 1890 cut logs manually, two men to a tree. Then the logs were taken to the mill on a small tram line. Note that these men are black. Although we have few photographs to show it, black residents were a vital part of the county's dream.

Only a few of these enormous logs could be transported at one time even with a "modern" truck like this. (Courtesy of Shirley Walker Meadows)

A loaded tram at the Grogan–Cochran Mill in 1926 illustrates an innovation which considerably streamlined the process of moving logs to the mill. These narrow gauge lines could be relocated to new cutting sites when necessary. (Courtesy of Celeste Graves)

While children lucky enough to have prosperous parents might dress as beautifully as Opal Grafft, daughters of mill workers had a much harder time of it. The Raymond girls must have had a mother who tried, though. She probably made their dresses by hand. Look at those bows! (Courtesy of Wanda Jordan)

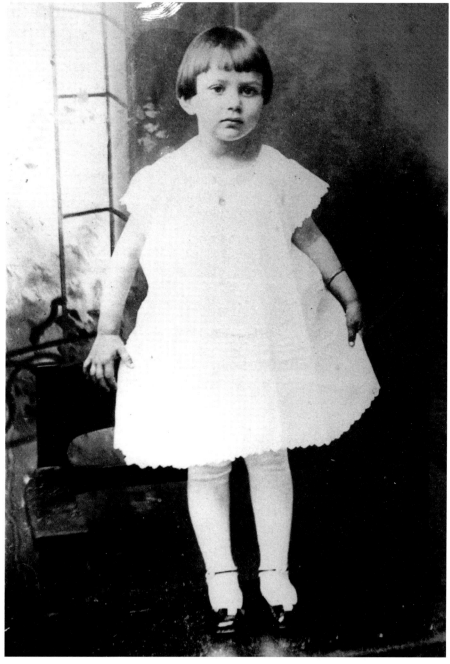

Each mill had its own currency to pay the workers. If you had worked at the Keystone Mill your pay would have looked like this. The round pieces were "chits" and the rectangular ones checks.

Homes provided for mill administrators were much more spacious and refined than those of the workers as seen in the home of B. C. Campbell at Waukegan in 1929. All mills were segregated not only racially but by rank and income.

RAILROADS

Railroads were more than a means of employment to this county. Almost from the beginning, the railroads had determined where growth would take place, which towns flourished and which withered. They gave us place-names, links to the larger world, markets, and accessibility for newcomers.

As early as 1870 the Willis brothers saw the potential and absolute necessity of railroads. They leased land on Mockingbird Hill to the Great Northern RR. This line (The International and Great Northern) was completed in 1872, offering North-South connections with Houston. During the early 1880s, the Santa Fe extended its lines to reach the county. In 1889 East-West service was established when the Gulf, Colorado, and Santa Fe Railroad crossed the IGN line at Conroe.

Other lines soon followed. Dacus benefited from the Chicago, Rock Island, and Pacific while Dobbin became a crossroad for this line and the

Before the actual railroads were laid survey crews prepared the way. J. W. Martin was crew boss for this team in 1910. (Courtesy of Bessie Owen)

Farmers loading produce at Honea Switch (c. 1905) had purchased "cut over" land from the Campbell Lumber Co. in small tracts. Because of the railroad they could load and ship to Chicago and other cities. Here all three of our major economies come together: farming, timber, and the railroad. (Courtesy of Mrs. Robert Clopton)

Gulf, Colorado and Santa Fe around 1900. Splendora, earlier on the old narrow-gauge Houston, East and West Texas RR now was on the Houston-Shreveport route of the Southern Pacific. While some towns resisted the coming of the railroads, most quickly saw their potential for growth. In fact, Montgomery residents decided to build their own in 1877 donating land, money, and labor. A charter was granted on December 31, 1877, and the Central and Montgomery RR Co. built a depot.

All towns of any size had a depot. Cedric Nutter recalls listening to the old engineers and conductors at the Conroe depot as they exchanged tales while waiting for a train. Cafes built near the depots became gathering spots, hotels and boarding houses clustered the area drawing their business primarily from rail travelers. Montgomery residents could catch the Santa Fe #217 to Conroe at 7:30 a.m., spend the day shopping, visiting, wheeling and dealing, and take the #218 home that evening at 8:30. Rather like a commuter flight to Dallas! Many used the train to go to Houston for a day—almost appealing if you've just had a bad day on I-45!

Trains and whistles were everywhere. Engineer Jack Butler (on a Conroe-Beaumont route) always arrived here around 9 p.m. The story goes he always began blowing his whistle at Stewart's Creek (1 1/2 miles East of Conroe) and didn't stop blowing until he reached the depot—his way of telling his wife to get dinner on! Meeting the train was not just something you did when a guest was expected. According to Cedric Nutter, the IG&N arrived each Sunday at 4:30 p.m. and meeting it was the "in" thing to do. He recalls that Uncle Nick Carregan who ran a local cafe with his wife Kate, once replied, when asked by

Creating those all important railroads was not exactly a "high–tech" operation in 1915. "Doc" and Lomas Chandler (second and third from the right) were from a family who had come here in 1869 in a wagon train from Florida. The other workers remind us that both white and black families provided our essential labor force. (Courtesy of Celeste Graves)

The signal tower at the Santa Fe, Trinity, and Brazos Valley RR crossing in Dobbin functioned much like an air control tower at an airport. (Courtesy of Bessie Owen)

No county resident was likely to miss seeing engines such as this one chugging through fields and towns with its "cowcatcher" leading the way and the caboose trailing along at the end of the train.

The depot was a central gathering spot in each town. Here in Magnolia in 1920 Station Agent W. J. Gayle, the one with the RR hat on, poses with some local citizens. (Courtesy of Celeste Graves)

a train passenger what the local population was, "Just count. They're all here."

Yes, railroads offered us much. Farmers could get their crops to profitable markets, the timber industry had a national market as well as tram-lines to make production more efficient, county residents had a means of travel, and county children had occasion to dream of far–off places when they heard those whistles blow.

But most dramatically the RR gave many people a chance to come here seeking their own dreams. These were not the Southern cotton planters who first came to the area but emigrant families from the East. The Heritage Museum has an old, very fragile brochure produced in 1878 by the IG&N RR. Its headline reads:

TEXAS WANTS ONE MILLION EMIGRANTS

The brochure then devotes a section to each of the forty counties on its train route. Of Montgomery County it says that it offers good farming lands, immense forests, fruit in abundance—especially wild grapes which "make an excellent quality of wine." In addition, the saw mills are mentioned and how affordable the cost of rough hewn timber was—$9 per thousand feet. It suggests that the largest and most important town is Willis (pop. 1,000) where land can be bought for $2.50–$3 per acre. "Here is a golden opportunity for manufacturers and capitalists."

Fares from St. Louis to Houston (First Class—$36.80, Emigrant—$21) make you wonder about the relative comfort of the accommodations. Also, a Prospector's fare was good for a round-trip if used within forty days. These tickets were bought, whole families relocating here to farm, work in the mills, and to open small businesses. A frequent event was the loading of an entire family—goods and all—onto a single boxcar, a "mobile home" of sorts, for the trip. Here they rode, often sitting in their own chairs and imagining their new destination. Upon arriving wagons would meet them at the train station and they too, became of the dream of Montgomery County.

ORDER PROHIBITING
USE OF
COMMON DRINKING CUP IN TEXAS

The use of a common drinking cup on railway trains and in railroad stations, is hereby prohibited from and after June 1, 1912. No person or corporation in charge of any of the aforesaid railway trains or railway stations, shall furnish any drinking cups for public use in said places, and no person or corporation shall permit on said railroad trains or in railroad stations the use of the drinking cup in common. There must also be posted in a conspicuous place by the individual or corporation, near the drinking water container mentioned in any of the foregoing paragraphs, a warning cardboard with this ruling printed thereon in large letters so it can be easily read.

(b) It shall be unlawful for any person to drink from the faucet or tap of any cooler, or drinking fountain, or other place where water is kept for human drink or consumption. The conductor of any train, or person in charge of any railway station, where is situated any cooler or drinking fountain, or other place where water is stored for human drink or consumption who shall allow drinking from the faucet or tap thereof, shall be deemed guilty of a violation of this ruling.

TEXAS STATE BOARD OF HEALTH,
Per RALPH STEINER, President

The widespread use of the railroad for passenger traffic sparked concern for health. In 1912 a law banning common drinking cups was enacted and this poster went up at all depots. (Courtesy of Bessie Owen)

OIL

In spite of all this industry, vision, and growth, Montgomery County, like the nation, suffered decline during the Depression. Markets for produce dwindled and the timber industry was ebbing in its productivity. But the county was blessed just at this moment with yet another economic boost—oil! For thirty years the county had been giving indications of its treasure and in 1901 a water well drilled by the Santa Fe Railroad contained oil traces. One man, Lowell Smith of Kansas, was such a true believer that each year he harvested his crops in Kansas and then spent the summer near Splendora trying well after well but none produced. Other wells were being drilled around Conroe while farmers often complained of gas seepage in their fields. Wells went in the Musgrove Field (6m. E) and the Top Shelf Field (5m.W) while at Tamina eighteen wells were drilled but all were abandoned. In 1914 a Santa Fe crew drilling for water found oil but the RR said to look elsewhere because they needed the water for their locomotives. An editorial of the time mused, "Why does no one pursue the quest?"

A few more did. A well located in the SE county looked promising in 1924 but was abandoned at 1,961 feet. Major oil companies, some of which had leased local land earlier, also gave up and turned back the leases. In 1929 the Kelley-Baker Field went as deep as 3,662 feet without success but by then funds for speculation were harder and harder to come by.

But George Strake had the same keen vision and deep commitment of those who had settled here one hundred years before. Born in 1894 in Saint Louis, Missouri, he had graduated from Saint Louis University, served in the Army Air Corps in W.W.I and was working for the Mexican-Gulf Oil Company in Tampico, Mexico. When the oil possibilities of Texas came to his

George Strake, his brother-in-law Wilt Pfiffner, and driller Harvey Lee at Discovery Well Strake #1. This well produced white casing head oil (diesel) unlike the pure crude oil Strake found at Strake #2 six months later.

George Strake and Pfiffner owed thanks to this drilling crew which brought in Strake #2. (Courtesy of Caroline Cryar)

Strake #2 came in on June 5, 1932. Although the first well is often recorded as the beginning of the boom, this one really convinced the oil industry of the county's importance. (Courtesy of Caroline Cryar)

attention, he moved here. Ignoring the local focus on the Kelley-Baker Field to the West, Strake withdrew all his savings and leased 8,500 acres 6 1/2 miles southeast of Conroe. Being only thirty six years old and with no clear "resume", Strake could find no outside funding but his test well began on August 3, 1931. After drilling deeper than any before him, he found gas sand but no conclusive results. He was out of money but so determined to succeed that he traded off some of his land to continue. At almost five thousand feet on December 13, 1931, George Strake's dream became a reality.

The effects were not as dramatic as we might think. *The Montgomery County News* four days later (December 17, 1931) reflects a rather conservative stance: " In any case...it means the spending of considerable sums of money here." George Strake had no doubts though and he quickly set up another rig, 2,400 feet away, and began drilling. On June 5, 1932 (at 5,026 feet) Strake #2 swept away all reservations about the area's oil-producing future, producing nine hundred barrels of "sweet crude" daily.

Now the oil boom was official. One estimate reports that Conroe grew from twenty five hundred to ten thousand in thirty days! Leasing was frenzied with some leases bringing $1,100 per acre for land which had originally been bought for about $10 per acre. Workers displaced by Depression lay-offs

This early rig on Lake Creek shows the board road allowing transport of the oil. The need for such roads revitalized our local timber business.

Always a breath taking moment—the blowout of a well. This one was at Crater Hill in the Conroe Field. Such a sight was the payoff for tedious drilling. Because of his experience with these frequent blowouts, Red Adair became a world famous firefighter. (Courtesy of Caroline Cryar)

flocked here seeking work—and finding it. For not only did the oil fields themselves need workers, but the ailing timber industry was revitalized by drillers' need for wooden derricks, lumber for roadways to the wells, and wood to fire boilers to operate the wells. Humble Oil bought 4,368 acres from Strake for $500,000 cash and $3,500,000 to be paid out of actual oil production.

The greatest development was in 1933. Fewer than one hundred wells were pumping 25,000 barrels daily early in the year but by year's end 679 wells were producing 52,500 barrels of crude oil per day. By 1938, the Conroe field alone had produced 77,063,000 barrels of oil and Conroe had become the third greatest oil-producing center in the United States.

Once again, a dream coupled with determination and hard work had brought Montgomery County into a new dimension. It is told of Strake that on that cold, raw and rainy day when Strake #1 blew in, he knelt in the mud and promised God that his church would share in this good fortune. In 1935 Strake did give a generous gift to the Sacred Heart Church in Conroe. Nor did he forget the community which had given him a home, workers, and friends. He was a charter member of the Conroe Rotary Club (August 4, 1932) and in 1943 gave 3,400 acres to the Boy Scouts for a camp which is still operating today.

Later technology developed processes to prevent such blowouts which often caused injury from fire. This crew is servicing such a piece of equipment. (Courtesy of Dolores Harrell)

George Kelley and Lawrence Tanner show us the working stock our county's success depended on. Both farmed, worked at the sawmills, on the railroads, and finally at Columbia Carbon after World War II. Their resumes would be a microcosm of the county's economic development. (Courtesy of Betty Holladay Kelley)

The Columbia Carbon Plant was actually opened in 1945 but serves to show us the continuing changes in our county's industry. This plant was especially helpful to returning veterans as it offered them jobs. (Courtesy of Wanda Jordan)

Making the Dream Available to All

As our earlier chapters clearly show, these first settlers were very busy folk. The "support systems" we so often rely on today were simply not available; they had to be resourceful and almost totally self-reliant. Building, farming, creating homes, and assuring food supplies—all of this took up their days and their resources. Right from the beginning they seemed to believe strongly that (as President Garfield put it) without public education, "neither justice nor freedom can permanently be maintained."

The earliest schools were basically a few hours spent in one settler's home with neighboring children often joining in and those adults who could "read and cipher" shared their knowledge with everyone. Land and buildings were often donated by citizens. For example, in 1837 Dr. Arnold and W. E. Clepper of Montgomery supplied land to the community for joint use as the public school and the Masonic Lodge. In the Magnolia area, the

Education in the county had come a long way by 1911 when this school in Magnolia was built but it never was left out by our early settlers. This school was replaced after a fire in 1926 adding more rooms, an auditorium, and a kitchen, but I wonder what happened to that bell and those steps over the wire fence? (Courtesy of Celeste Graves)

113

Many early schools were supported by (or housed in) local churches. This 1905 school picture is in front of either the Baptist or the Methodist Church in Magnolia. In 1911 Magnolia built its own school. (Courtesy of Celeste Graves)

The Waukegan School served about three hundred pupils in 1926. Ethel Anderson, the teacher, certainly had to have flexible lesson plans to reach the many age levels in this one class. The dog looks as posed and orderly as the class! (Courtesy of Wanda Jordan)

first of two schools was located at the Farmer's Grange Hall and the second school at the Methodist Church. Since the first was near the Baptist Church, they were locally designated the Baptist and the Methodist schools, but they were not church schools and students chose whichever they preferred.

Later more schools were established, some with full-time teachers. There is an 1842 note of an "English and Classical School" near Montgomery with Rev. P. H. Fullenwider as the teacher. The Montgomery Academy was created in 1848 in a two-story log house. The Jones Academy had both boarding and non-boarding students until the Civil War when Mr. Jones' son and most of the older boys went off to war. After the war the building was rented to two returning soldiers, Alexander Boyd and T. J. Peel, who reopened the school. The first Conroe area school was opened in 1886 at Conroe's Mill with Miss Ione Burns as the teacher. Willis students first used the Danville school (c. 1859–1860) then attended a one-room school called Bedrock. A private school, the Willis Male and Female College, began in 1888 and ran until 1901 when it was sold to Willis for use as a public school.

Conditions were spartan at these early schools. Semesters ran short because of farming needs and/or a lack of funds. The McRae School (fifteen miles East of Conroe) began in October after the harvest was done and shut down in March for planting season. But you can be sure teachers such as Miss Ruth Cable taught these students well. At the Montgomery Academy, some pupils brought their own chairs and tables while others sat at long narrow benches and worked at a common desk. The Sam Ashe School (south of Tamina Road) boasted a pump outside, an outdoor toilet with two seats and a ventilation pipe, as recalled by Ruby Barrow.

At the Mill Creek Singing School near Magnolia, students could receive music instruction for $1 a week. This group of "singing scholars" pose c. 1912. (Courtesy of Celeste Graves)

The Harmony Community near Montgomery had its own school in 1906.
Given the location there were surely some Weisingers and Musgroves among
this class.

A typical country school, the Kidd School (on FM 1314 SE of Conroe) was a
one room school house with one teacher. The children either walked or rode a
wagon to school. (Courtesy of Shirley Walker Meadows)

The school in Dobbin was built by K. W. Faulks who did much of the local construction during the 1920s. (Courtesy of Bessie Owen)

The J. O. H. Bennette School was the first brick school in Conroe (1911–1912). It sat at the end of Main Street where the swimming pool is now. (Courtesy of Thelma Hicks)

D. A. Franks was principal of the Willis Male and Female College around the turn of the century. (Courtesy of Bessie Owen)

None of the education was free or state subsidized in those early years. At the Willis Male and Female College, tuition was $2-$5 per month (depending on whether one studied music) or $175 per term, including board. At one time some two hundred fifty students boarded there. After classes, a bell rang to signal two to three hours of supervised study in a large hall. At the Conroe Normal and Industrial College (opened in 1903), Dr. Jimmie Johnson and his wife Chaney ran a school situated on one hundred five acres. Here cottages and dorms supplied housing; the men farmed while women worked in the kitchen and laundry. All were neatly dressed; the men in coats and ties, the women in black skirts and white middies. In Conroe around 1897, one hundred thirty two pupils attended college. Some of them boarded in private homes for $10 a week but many relied on what could be brought from home, typically cold biscuits and maybe a cold baked sweet potato.

Sadly, our Negro children did not find education very accessible but by the turn of the century some provisions were being made. The first public school for blacks was built in Conroe in 1911 and called Campbell High School. Before that, classes had been held at the Central Baptist Church in the Madeley Quarters. The eleven-room school (between Ave. K and M) became the Booker T. Washington School in 1931. In 1939 George Washington Carver School in the old Conroe-Magnolia Road section served the Magnolia area students, grades one through seven while high school students were bused to Montgomery. In 1903 Dr. Jimmie Johnson sought to provide further education for black people and through personal sacrifice and extensive solicitation of funds, managed to open Conroe Normal and Industrial College on one hundred five acres of land. Here students from their late teens to adulthood could come to study, prepare for professional careers or learn a useful trade. They lived here, working on the school farm or in the laundry

The Willis Male and Female College, although the name is misleading, taught students only through high school.

house and sometimes accepting local jobs to supplement their income. No student was turned away for lack of tuition. The women wore black skirts and white middy blouses; the men, a coat and tie always. Every student took courses in Bible and Christian education regardless of what they studied. Students came from all over, many drawn by the performances of the college's male quartet which traveled to promote the college. The school grew under the leadership of Dr. Davis Abner and Dr. William Johnson, serving over four hundred students around 1920. However, the Depression took its toll. Dr. Johnson had to preach for money to feed his students and faculty However, enrollment never again regained its earlier size.

Concerned citizens had to supply any "frills" for these schools. For example in Magnolia, c. 1901, the local school had no library until Wilora Thomas sold magazine subscriptions to fund one. In Conroe, students sold subscriptions to buy stained glass windows for the auditorium of the J. O. H. Bennette School in 1911. (These were later moved to the new Crockett High School.) Another hurdle was simply getting to school! There were none of the distinctive yellow buses we take for granted today. Most children walked around two miles to reach their school. It was not until the turn of the century that some area schools offered transportation. In the Splendora area, a wagon picked up students. W. E. Williams, a trustee of the McRae School, "fathered" the concept of school bus routes in 1925. The bus was a Model-T Ford. In 1930, Sam Godsey modified a truck, adding seats and curtains in the windows, to create one of Conroe's first buses. Children rode in open-sided cars, thirty to thirty-five to a bus in the Willis bus fleet. They sat on wooden seats and could lower canvas curtains if rain or cold required it. Some children who missed the bus might be able to get to the railroad track and catch the "doodle bug" into school.

Mary Enloe and Nettie McKibben were students at the Willis Male and Female College. Their attire is a far cry from that of today's students. (Courtesy of Rosamond Strozier)

The Montgomery Academy began in a two-story log building but had moved to this building by 1870.

The influx of new students brought on by the oil boom created a need for larger schools. In 1935 Sam Houston Elementary in Conroe was built on ten acres of land donated by S. K. Hailey and paid for with taxes from the oil field.

This second grade class at Bennette School in Conroe in 1930–1931 was taught by Garnet Evans.

New facilities such as this 1938 gym in Magnolia brought pride and a place to accommodate local events to many communities. (Courtesy of Celeste Graves)

Though early students walked or rode wagons to school, by the mid-1920s schools sometimes offered busses. The driver of this Magnolia bus must have found time for a bit of fishing! (Courtesy of Celeste Graves)

Willis students could catch a ride on a bus from this fleet in 1926. Drivers were paid $30 a month and free tuition for their children. Russ Clanton was a relief driver for this fleet. (Courtesy of Russ Clanton)

Iola Everett, later to become Mrs. T. E. Gentry, taught speech in Conroe c. 1919. I bet it was called Elocution! (Courtesy of Anne Moore)

The Conroe High School faculty in the 1920s with "Skipper" Anderson in the back center. (Courtesy of Caroline Cryar)

Early in the new century the state began to provide funds for county schools—$1.75 per pupil. When the money was depleted, the school simply closed, often after only four or five months. Yet citizens persevered, finding ways to shoulder the cost of education. In 1899 Conroe residents paid a tax of twenty-five cents on each $100 in order to build a new four-room school on the site where old Travis Junior High was located. From this school the first graduating class, three women and one man, proudly heard the commencement address given by Miss Eva Talley in 1902. Montgomery County chose to find the funds to employ a County Superintendent to coordinate its programs even before the state required such leadership.

Many fine educators served our schools in those years, but the vision and the vitality which kept them going through boom and depression is perfectly embodied in Hulon N. Anderson who served the Conroe Ind. School District for forty one years. Anderson was a native of Montgomery County, "born and raised" at Willis. There he taught at the Willis Male and Female College, served as Supt. of the Teague schools, and came to CISD as its "Skipper" in 1905. He was not a remote manager nor a bureaucrat for he taught every subject except Latin and was directly involved in all facets of education here. When funds ran short he personally solicited local businessmen for supplemental money to help his educational programs.

Mr. Anderson began his innovative career by cleaning and whitewashing the interiors of all the rural schools. Then he placed a box at the front door of each school to collect donated books. The first two books in the Conroe school library were a tonic almanac and a French novel but at least we had a

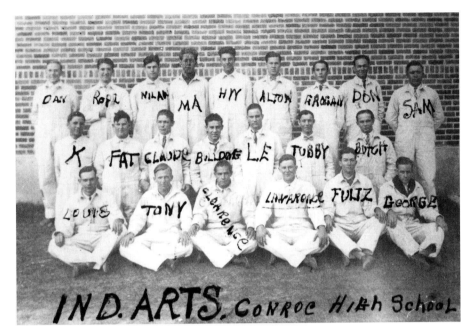

Schools provided "book learning" but also gave important vocational skills such as those learned by this Industrial Arts class in Conroe in the 1920s.

Schools provided pride and competition, too. May Queen Katherine Massingale of Magnolia High School in 1928 and her court: Ruth Gale, Sadie Hicklin, Ema Yon, Jean Massingale, and Eulene Johnson are as proud as any Miss Universe lineup. (Courtesy of Celeste Graves)

Basketball was also popular. This Willis team of 1926 look young but determined. They played on an outside dirt court. Coached by D. B. Sherman they beat Conroe twice that year! (Courtesy of Russ Clanton)

A typical football player of 1920 Carson Uzzell was part of a long tradition of football at Conroe High School. (Courtesy of Caroline Cryar)

As early as 1907 the schools placed emphasis on sports. Here, Conroe's baseball team poses with a few of its rooters. (Courtesy of Caroline Cryar)

In 1930 Magnolia High School won both boy's and girl's county championships in basketball. (Courtesy of Celeste Graves)

Students learned life skills, too! At Conroe, any boy who came to school with unshined shoes had to pay a nickel to the school fund for a shine. Skipper Anderson insisted shirts had to be tucked in and collars buttoned and only in World War II did he agree to allow young girls to wear anklets rather than hose.

library! He encouraged the students and faculty to help out. Homemaking classes made and sold jam from mayhaw berries (gathered by the boys) to a cafe in Detroit for fifty cents a half-pint, waste paper was baled and sold to a Houston company, and the shop classes contracted for local carpenter work. As a result of such leadership, in 1911–1912 we built the first brick school, the Bennette School. When the new Crockett High School was built in 1927, Skipper was right there supervising the move which was carried out by the faculty and students. In 1935 he installed the first school cafeteria at Sam Houston Elementary School. Before that teachers had made soup on the classroom stoves using whatever ingredients the students had been able to bring from home that day. Although this soup was intended for those whose families had not been able to supply lunch, rumor has it that the aroma of the simmering pot was so appealing that several students "lost" the brown bag lunches that Mama had so carefully prepared that morning!

Yes, Skipper Anderson's energy and determination along with that of countless others, gave the young of this county a chance to study, to play, to be involved in activities as diverse as forensics, football, home economics, history, shop, and science. In short, education gave the new generations their own dreams and enabled them to achieve those dreams.

Of course all those winning teams were ably supported by the band. In Conroe, Betty Stinson led the Marching Band in the late 1940s. (Courtesy of Betty Stinson Gowing)

At Magnolia High football was the six-man kind until 1947. In 1941 this team won the state championship. (Courtesy of Celeste Graves)

Cheerleaders and pep squads brought even more students into the sports activities. This group at Magnolia in 1941 created school spirit at every sports event. (Courtesy of Celeste Graves)

Some went on to college. A dorm room at Sam Houston State in 1913 shows local coeds at leisure. Banners suggest their hometowns or other colleges where their "sweethearts" might be attending. Myrtle Anderson (second from the left) seems focused on that card game! (Courtesy of John and Sarah Gibson)

With their education done, graduates like Hart Addison (1909, on the left) went on to contribute to their community as richly as they had drawn from it.

Cam Harrell sums up the fruits of education here. As a young man he studied at Conroe High School earning the nickname Powder for his football skills. He was a key player on the 1937 team coached by Joe Lagow and Mac McCullough which won the Texas quarter-finals. His academics (right), his sports, his military service as a pilot (left), and his career as a lawyer in Conroe (below, second from left)—stories such as his are what education is all about in Montgomery County. (Courtesy of Dolores Harrell)

Keeping the Dream Lofty

In the midst of, indeed at the heart of all of this ground-breaking, building, and growth was the faith of our fathers. From the beginning, as each community sprang up, they sought to provide schools and churches for themselves and their children. They knew their dreams must be kept lofty if they were to survive the hardships of this new life. At first there were no church houses or full time ministers. Most communities met for worship in a private home or under a brush arbor (an open shelter supported by four by six poles covered with palmetto leaves or other foliage with a sawdust floor.) Here they gathered to hear the word brought by the circuit riders.

These circuit riders were the main stay of all of our early congregations, appearing once or twice a month. Each rider might have as many as five or six churches to serve. We read of services held by a "missionary" out of Nacogdoches on a six-week circuit in 1838. Another early record remembers a Brother Z. N. Morrell, a Baptist who called himself a "cane-brake preacher." In 1839 an appeal went back to the United States for help in acquiring ministers. One man in Georgia, Jesse Mercer, gave $2,500 to send William Tryon to the area while the Methodists sent Isaac Strickland to "organize" the churches in this area.

Strickland was effective and because of his efforts and the zeal of the residents churches began to develop. In

The Piney Grove Methodist–Episcopal Church was built in Mink around 1887. Before this the congregation met in a one room church on land donated by the Morrow family, sitting on backless benches to hear two hour sermons by circuit riders. (Courtesy of Celeste Graves)

The church was the center of life and death for many cemeteries were in or near churchyards. The church kept records and old gravemarkers such as this one speak eloquently of the pain and sacrifice of the early settlers. On one side Mary Linton, who died in 1871 at age forty four and on the other the three children whom she had lost. Dreams have a high cost!

Montgomery, a piece of land had been set aside for a church in 1838. Not only did a church rise in 1842 but the first parsonage ever built in Texas went up as well with the church bell being supplied by the Willis brothers. Buried in the church cemetery are four of the early circuit riders, a fitting resting place for those who were so much a part of our early growth. In 1844 a church was created in Post Oak Grove (seven miles west of Montgomery) and in 1850 the Bay's Chapel Church was organized. Also in 1850, the Macedonia Baptist Church occupied a building in Magnolia near the W.O.W. hall which later became the First Baptist Church. The Mill Creek Church of Christ met in the school until 1922 when it actually took over the building.

Of course, many of these churches still relied on circuit riders. As late as 1870 a Rev. South from Bryan preached once a month to area Methodists. Sometimes local men preached as well as holding down other jobs. In 1891 Rev. W. B. Shannon preached at three area churches: Union Grove (28 members), Conroe (20), and Arnold's Mill (4). Rev. Nutter, after working all week, preached on weekends at Montgomery, Phelps, Harmony, and Spring in 1894 and the Rev. Hollis Williams of Dobbin farmed, was a blacksmith and notary, preached, played the violin and hand-saw! These men needed to be versatile as churches had few funds for salary. The Danville Baptists, for example, were able to pay Rev. J. V. Wright only $175 a year. Because they were so much a part of the life of the people, faith was an all-week presence. The pastor at Willis in 1862 was N. T. Byars, who had been Sam Houston's blacksmith. In fact, the Texas Declaration of Independence had been signed in his blacksmith shop.

Like their ministers, church members were resourceful and willing to go to great lengths for their faith. Most of the early churches were built on land donated by a member and paid for by local gifts. When the Conroe Methodists

The Reverend G. M. Daniel and his wife Sarah Elizabeth served the Willis and then the Conroe Methodist church from 1891 to 1896. Their values contributed much to our county and to the state. One son, M. P. Daniel, published the *Willis Progress* and his other son, Price Daniel, served as a governor of Texas. (Courtesy of Doris Daniel)

In December 1850 Thomas Bay and his wife built a log home and then a log building to be used as a school and a church—with six members. In the early 1870s a new frame building on the same site served as both school and church. This is the back view of Bay's Chapel as it looked in 1900.

The Methodist Church in Conroe
met first in a small school house and
in 1891 built this church on land
given by Isaac Conroe. Their first
preacher was Rev. W. B. Shannon.
(Courtesy of Caroline Cryar)

METHODIST CHURCH CONROE TEX

needed a building, thirty-three men pledged $418.50 to build on a lot given by Isaac Conroe. The women made the altar linens, baked the communion bread, and made wine from grapes picked from a vine at the Nutter home. The Willis Methodists advertised for—and received—gifts of seats, lamps, a Bible, and hymnals for their new church in 1879. Its pews and railings were made by E. A. Anderson, Capt. Smith donated the steeple bell, and the pulpit was made at the prison in Huntsville. When the Conroe Church of Christ moved to a building at 320 Collins, Mrs. Vera McComb heard of a communion set—sixteen cups and a few trays—for sale in Huntsville and drove there in her little Ford to purchase it for the church. Thereafter, Mrs. J. A. Hanna baked unleavened bread for each communion service.

These churches for which they had worked so diligently were central to their lives. They gathered for worship usually three times a week—Sunday morning, evening and on Wednesday for Prayer Meetings. They attended Sunday School classes, held revivals, gospel meetings, and rejoiced in baptisms with these events often being held outdoors. We read of many baptisms at Mule Lot Hole on Mill Creek. At one such baptism Mack Winslow, a Bible reader but an independent, surprised the faithful when he appeared on his horse, dismounted, walked fully clothed into the creek and presented himself for baptism. These events were often considered newsworthy. In a *Conroe Courier* column about Magnolia (9/15/11) we read that a month-long revival had concluded with "nine baptisms—and all revived in religion." Churches were indeed the hubs of the communities for it was in the Montgomery Baptist Church that a major debate over Texas' secession took place between Sam Houston and J. P. Wiley.

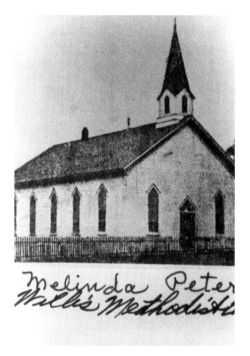

The Willis Methodist Church originally in Danville moved here in 1877, meeting in a schoolhouse until this church was completed in 1879. Its pastors then were G. S. Sandel and J. M. Pugh.

After sharing a building with the Methodists for four years the Conroe Baptist Church was able to move to this site on South First and Avenue E in 1895. Reverend Daniel preached the first sermon here. (Courtesy of Doris Daniel)

By the turn of the century the old building had grown too small. After years of planning and effort the Conroe Baptists completed this building in 1921. The old building was sold to a black congregation who later returned it and the material became part of an eight room education building in 1922. (Courtesy of Dortha Altman)

The churches in return responded to the needs of their community. Records of the Waverly Presbyterian Church in 1863 show that provisions were made for the admission to membership of those black members who are "servants of our white members." As mills and mill towns appeared, new churches arose. When Grogan/Cochran bought Lone Star Lumber in 1928, they built a church for employees—the Alethia Baptist Church. In the 1920s, A. E. Hickerson of Delta Land, Co. and A. W. Runyan, principal of Conroe High School, cooperated together to offer a Sunday School class for mill workers who came directly from work. This class grew so large it had to move to the courthouse and took the name "Runyan's Roughnecks." In 1932 a Mexican Baptist Church was established on the Grogan Sawmill grounds. The new immigrants, drawn by the mills and later the oil fields, also created a need for growth of the Catholic Church which had long been listed as a mission of first, the Plantersville and secondly, the Waverly Catholic churches. The oil boom and resulting camps saw even more growth, as in Mims Baptist Church established at the Humble Camp in 1932.

What we clearly see here is a total unity between work and worship, between surviving and sustaining life. These people understood that land, business, education, and religion were all essential fibers in the tapestry of their dream.

In 1916 the Conroe Methodists sold the old building for $500 and moved to Main and Phillips where the new church, costing $11,208 was completed in 1917. (Courtesy of Dortha Altman)

The church provided worship, records, and recreation! This Methodist Sunday School picnic on May 1, 1901, in Conroe enjoyed quite a turnout. Look at those hats! (Courtesy of Caroline Cryar)

The Montgomery Baptist Church built in 1901 is now owned by the Montgomery Historical Society which opens it every April and December for visitors. Also, weddings and receptions may be scheduled here.

The Baptist Women's Missionary Society (formed in 1904) was a powerful force in church and community endeavors. Here they meet in 1921. The donor's mother, Mrs. J. L. Hicks is fifth from the left on the third row. (Courtesy of Dr. Paul Hicks)

Church members participated in all areas of church life. Adults as well as children attended Sunday School classes such as these at the Security Baptist Church c. 1903. The donor's grandmother, Cora Alice Walker (center with white hat) and her grandfather Wesley Ira Walker were members. (Courtesy of Shirley Walker Meadows)

The Magnolia Baptist Church was first named the Macedonia Church of Mink Prairie. When the town moved in 1909 the old church was torn down and its material used to build this church completed in 1912. Ansel Steger was a leader in the church. No—the cow was not one of the congregation! But note that church and day-to-day life never were far apart back then. (Courtesy of Celeste Graves)

The growth of churches was sparked by tent revivals such as this one in Magnolia in 1926. It was a joint effort of Methodists and Baptists. Such revivals often lasted as long as two weeks. (Courtesy of Celeste Graves)

Yes, the church did much to keep our dream lofty and to pass it on—as in the Hicks family, always an important part of the Baptist Church and of the community. Four generations are seen here celebrating the groundbreaking for the Baptist Church in Conroe. (Dr. Paul Hicks, second from right.)

Churches were involved in community life in those days. Here Montgomery church takes part in a Temperance Parade in 1918.

Notice to the Public

NO LOAFING
In Montgomery County

Under direction of the UNITED STATES Authorities, all Peace Officers are being called upon to take action looking to the elimination of all Idleness and Loafing of all able-bodied persons in every town and community.

In furtherance of this suggestion the slogan of Montgomery County shall be:

GO TO WAR,
GO TO WORK, or
Go to Jail.

Very Respectfully,

M. A. ANDERSON, Sheriff,
Montgomery County, Texas

CHAPTER SEVEN

Keeping the Dream Free

Only in dreams do dreams come true without cost. The dream of our early settlers was paid for not only in hard work and sacrifice here in the county, but with military service when that dream was threatened. Although they had been "invited" to come here by land grants, the Mexican law of April 6, 1830, prohibited further colonization and Mexico sent troops to collect customs. When Patrick Jack and William B. Travis protested these impositions, they were arrested. In 1831 an army of one hundred sixty men led by John Austin gathered near Liberty to secure their release. Among them was J. H. Shepperd of Montgomery. Finally, the Battle of Velasco rid the Anglo-American areas of these troops. Allen Larrison of Hi-Point was there as was Strap Buckner, a casualty of the encounter.

Stephen Austin and his "peace party" tried to negotiate at the 1832 Convention of San Felipe, but their grievances were ignored. Then in 1833, with Wharton's "war party" in ascendancy, a second Convention was held with Sam Houston as Chairman. A Constitution was finally drafted. Among those attending from Montgomery were William Robinson, Jared Groce, Joshua Hadley, and Jessie Grimes.

In 1835 when war actually erupted, Montgomery County was very much involved. In October at Mission Concepcion, Joseph Bennett, S. H. Shepperd, and Matthew Cartwright along with ninety other Texians faced four

If anyone doubted Montgomery County's commitment to both hard work and to keeping the dream free, this poster should set him straight.

Typical of this devotion to duty is Capt. Franklin Goldstein Dupree of Magnolia. He organized a company of cavalry, DeBray's regulars, which fought for four years in the Civil War. But his real love was hunting, fishing, his eight children, his farm and his sawmill. In 1892 he also served as justice of the peace for Precinct Number Three.
(Courtesy of Celeste Graves)

hundred Mexican soldiers. W. S. Taylor of Montgomery recalled the "Grass Fight" at Old Mill Creek in November where S. H. Shepperd and G. W. Robinson also fought. As hostile forces threatened, the Governor Henry Smith noted "the alarming fact that the enemy . . . is about to attack our beloved country at all points and the unorganized and deplorable conditions of the military". This prompted him to designate J. G. W. Pierson as *aide d' camp* to mobilize the District of Viesca (the name given this area in an earlier survey).

Even at the Alamo our citizens were numbered. John Goodrich, Charles Grimes, and Jonathan Lindley of Danville unfortunately died there while others narrowly escaped with their lives. Capt. Allen Larrison (who sold grog at Pierson's store in Hi-Point) had organized a relief force which did not arrive in time. However Sam Houston used such forces well in the campaign leading to San Jacinto. All of the Second Company of the Second Regiment were from this county. At San Jacinto the Cartwrights of Bear Bend, G. W. Robinson of Montgomery, and J. L. Bennett of Hi-Point fought. Bennett had brought a troop of eleven men and later was named Lt. Colonel of the 2nd Regiment of Texas Volunteers. It was John M. Wade who, on the march there, christened the two cannons the "Twin Sisters." Our county claims the first casualty of that battle, George Lamb, and the last survivor, Alphonso Steele. W. S. Taylor was actually there for the capture of Santa Anna!

Although the war ended, the hostilities did not. In 1842 when Mexican forces led by General Adrian Woll occupied San Antonio, General Alexander Somerville organized a Texas army of two regiments. J. L. Bennette of this county commanded one of them, and Nat Davis was also in that regiment. The army got to Bexar, but in December Somerville aborted the mission and most returned home. Some soldiers that did remain pursued the Mexican force to Meir but were captured. One out of ten was shot and the others were sent to Perote Prison. Young Robert Holmes Dunham was one of those executed and Leonidas Sanders, who had been Chief Justice of this county, later died at the prison.

For a few decades, citizens could once again plant, build, and dream their dreams. Many here worked to promote annexation. On May 10, 1845, a mass meeting was held here to promote the plan. But with statehood, we became part of the problems leading to the Civil War. Although slavery was certainly central to our economy (in 1860, 2,106 slaves were on record here) secession was not universally desired. In June 1861, two hundred eight county citizens drafted a petition against the idea, but their protest was to no avail.

When the war came, we were in the ranks. Montgomery County was divided into 5 "beats" with a home guard in each. Some of them were the Montgomery County Rifle Boys, led by Major Israel Worsham, Capt. R. O. Oliver's Company, Capt. Wooldridge's Mounted Rifles, and Terry's Texas Rangers of Plantersville. Recruitment was spirited. Bell's Grove Plantation near Montgomery was a Confederate recruiting center and Proctor Porter recruited throughout the area, organizing Company H. By the end of the war that Company had lost sixty-seven men, forty-seven were wounded and only nine came home alive. Not only soldiers but gun powder came from here. A major Confederate powder mill was located on Spring Creek until 1863, when an explosion shut it down. A historical marker in Spring Creek Park denotes its site.

Our forefathers fought well, always keeping in mind their dream of returning to build this county. For example, Col. Henry Marshall Elmore organized and commanded the 20th Regiment of Texas Volunteers, posted in Galveston to protect the port from Union ships which shelled the beach. Because they were sometimes in steam-boats, they were called the "horse marines" and some called this the "Featherbed Regiment" because it was thought to be an easy post. But Col. Elmore's eldest son was killed in the Battle of the Wilderness and one of his privates, Willis F. Cude, was captured and imprisoned. Escaping from Jackson, Miss., he walked for sixteen days to return to his duty, stopping in Houston to replace his worn-out shoes. He charged the new pair to Jeff Davis! Captain T. J. Peel of Montgomery who had studied at Austin College (then in Huntsville) fought in the battles of Shiloh and Chickamauga, then rode his horse three weeks to return to his county. Others too, brought back memories. Uncle Nick Carnegan, a Confederate bugler, blew mess call every day at noon and Taps every evening at 9 p.m. in front of his cafe.

The women, too, suffered. Elizabeth Spiller (Arnold Smith's grandmother) remembers a night of terror when their home near Danville was occupied by Yankee soldiers, forcing her mother and the three small children to hide. Fortunately, they left the next day, taking with them only the food.

James Matthew Gary of Montgomery was proud to wear this Confederate uniform when he felt duty called but was glad to return home to run a boarding house. This home still stands near Caroline and #149. (Courtesy of Bessie Owen)

Major and Mrs. C. R. Scott at their home in Montgomery shared many memories. He was the last Confederate veteran from Montgomery. (Courtesy of Bessie Owen)

Young men such as Ores Fultz (right) shared tents like this one, as well as a commitment to liberty in World War I. (Courtesy of Gary Calfee)

This unit was sent to France in 1918. Prince Simonton (standing second from left) was from Montgomery. (Courtesy of Katy Dean Hill)

Our local National Guard (1917) in front of the courthouse was led by second Lieutenant Bart Hawkins. After World War I, the practice of creating a unit all from one area was discontinued so that in the event of disaster the loss would not be so devastating.

Edmond Wooldridge of Willis returned to marry Lois Conroe.

Harold Godsey looked very young in this World War I uniform but was proud to volunteer to protect his dream! (Courtesy of Shirley Walker Meadows)

Reconstruction here, as elsewhere, was a time of trouble and racial conflict. Black citizens, though free, were destitute for lack of work. Those leaders who tried to help by seeking elective office were often victims of Ku Klux Klan violence. Around 1870 one such leader was elected to the Congress but was killed by the Klan. These same terrorists worked to discourage any political participation among the black community and were suspected to be the agents of several deaths and disappearances of black teachers as well. Records speak of one such person: William McGrew who was a Republican, civil servant, horse thief and a klansman.

Nevertheless, Montgomery County had enough sane citizens to weather these times, to prosper again, and to nurture in our young the sense that freedom must be fought for and preserved if dreams were to come true. A Mrs. Mildred Johnson of this county contended that she raised her children in the principles of two books: George Washington's *Rules of Conduct* and Pennypacker's *History of the Texas Revolution*. When World War I began, many from Montgomery County went even before they were called. A troop train was loaded and ready to leave the Waukeghan Depot on November 11, 1918 when they received word of the Armistice. Again in 1941 our citizens were there to serve. Even today, this tradition runs deep. Astronaut Robert Crippen learned his early values right here in Porter. The dream of freedom truly is contagious!

Gary Williams, son of Judge Williams fought for freedom in World War I and then returned to become postmaster in Conroe for thirty years from 1935 to 1965. (Courtesy of Suzie Williams Brignac)

Edward Matthews of Magnolia joined the army the minute war was declared in 1917. Twenty-six others from the area followed his example. (Courtesy of Celeste Graves)

Some of our young men served in both World War I and World War II. Lieutenant Thomas Earl Gentry stayed in the Reserves after 1918 and saw action in the next war, retiring as a Major. He also served us well as Conroe City Councilman, Fire Chief (1924–1930), and Mayor (1930–1942, 1948–1950). Again we see the clear awareness that the dream required service of all kinds. (Courtesy of Mrs. A. L. Moore)

World War II drew soldiers from every area of the county. Our black citizens too, contributed to the defense of the dream—even if it had been so long denied to them. J. W. Johnson and Robert Davis were among the Magnolia men who served. Note the overseas cap worn by Robert Davis. (Courtesy of Celeste Graves)

Not all joined the Army. Edgar Yon chose to serve in the U. S. Navy during World War I. (Courtesy of Celeste Graves)

During WWII Montgomery County had a U. S. Naval Base. Why? Well, Hitler very much wanted the white casing head oil produced here (he even sent agents to contract for all we could send.) So when we became involved in the war, the government created this base to protect against such. The base was called an R and R base for naval airmen. After the war ended in Europe the site became our county airport, still a major source of revenue for the county today. These pictures were taken at an open–house for the public in 1945. The glamorous woman with the flight scarf is Martha Welschaus, donor of the photographs.

Celebrating the Dream

These early settlers clearly worked, studied, and worshipped to achieve their dream yet they knew how to find a bit of fun when time allowed. On such occasions they came together to celebrate life, to share their accomplishments, to enjoy.

Most early recreation was at home and closely tied to farming life. A house-raising usually meant a picnic afterwards. Nutting parties in the fall, canning sessions, quilting bees, taffy-pulls, and hog-butcherings—all combined work and play. Of course in the evenings they read the Bible but sometimes one of the monthly magazines like Happy Hours or Good Stories would be read. Dominos or checkers, often played on a homemade board with buttons was another activity relished by family members.

When they did get a chance to get out, it was often to large halls such as the Recreation Hall at Waukegan or John Sallee's Dance Hall at Splendora. There square-dancing, box-suppers, and ice-cream socials gave pleasure to the entire family. Outside the hall, horseshoe pitching or a

Our citizens realized that all that hard work had to be seasoned and celebrated with some joy. Here Jack King, Edd McGee, and Lloyd Boardsman relax after a day of bridge building with an impromptu jam session in the cool of the evening. (Courtesy of Dortha Altman)

Everyone tried fishing. Young Sam Hailey (in the white hat) has a big one but his friends look disappointed. (Courtesy of Steve Hailey)

The Godsey family had a great day on May 25, 1925, catching twenty-three pounds all together. Back then recreation was also a means of providing food. (Courtesy of Shirley Walker Meadows)

Because hunting was so important, many families kept "coon dogs" such as these belonging to the Alfords of Magnolia.
(Courtesy of Celeste Graves)

Frank Dean, Sr., was a duck hunter—evidently a good one! He relaxed this way after working at Dean, Bros., a general store he and his brothers organized in 1902.

A buggy ride was a favorite outing. These Willis young people, c. 1923, may have been heading for a box supper or a picnic. (Courtesy of Jesse Traylor)

Traveling shows and county fairs were special events for the community. This tent was bought from a circus which went broke here. Jack King used it to camp when he was on bridge building jobs. (Courtesy of Dortha Altman). The fairs gave local residents the chance to show off their produce and handicrafts. (Courtesy of Shirley Walker Meadows)

A game of dominoes entertains Dobbin men in front of Hester Hawkin's place, c. 1936. (Courtesy of Bessie Owens)

Everyone had a favorite swimming hole. Mule Lot Hole was a popular one near Magnolia. Here Thelma Gage and Pearl Hydrick model the latest in swimwear in 1923. (Courtesy of Celeste Graves)

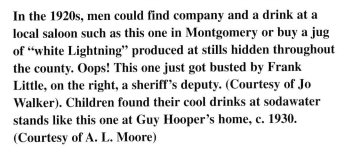

In the 1920s, men could find company and a drink at a local saloon such as this one in Montgomery or buy a jug of "white Lightning" produced at stills hidden throughout the county. Oops! This one just got busted by Frank Little, on the right, a sheriff's deputy. (Courtesy of Jo Walker). Children found their cool drinks at sodawater stands like this one at Guy Hooper's home, c. 1930. (Courtesy of A. L. Moore)

CONROE TEX.

CORNER DRUG STORE

AVE. Z.

Children enjoyed "hanging out at the tracks" to meet the trains as did Calvin and Marie Uzzell, c. 1906 (Courtesy of Caroline Cryar). But they also looked forward to special events such as watermelon feasts (Courtesy of Shirley Walker Meadows), Easter Egg hunts (Courtesy of Anna Lee Ramey), and school picnics like this one at Stewart Creek in 1901.

Not frequent—but surely a rare moment of leisure—snow! Here Lula Duke, her daughter Lovie Worsham, and Billie Bob enjoy the luxury of a snowman. (Courtesy of Gary Calfee)

Other thrills were provided by airshows like Pop Gaither's barnstorming tours. Cecil Beyette, on the left, of Magnolia flew on these as well as doing tours to demonstrate that rice could be seeded from the air.
(Courtesy of Celeste Graves)

Local baseball teams drew big crowds. In 1920 the Splendora team was reputed to be the best in the county but by the 1930s competition grew stiffer. The Strake Wildcats and the Fostoria Lumberjacks were often rivals and fierce loyalties existed. These teams played in real parks such as Lewis Park in Conroe which was built on ten acres given to them by Judge John L. Lewis and built by local volunteers.

In 1933, Conroe had its first Boy Scout Troop with Scoutmasters Eddie
Stephan, on the left, and Mickey Sims to teach them.
(Courtesy of Meta Stephan)

This large group gathered for a county fox hunt was held where the airport now stands. They had to import the foxes! (Courtesy of Caroline Cryar)

Our residents found time to celebrate the dream, whether it be in sports, play, or social clubs like this Ladies Social Club which Mary Agnes Wahrenberger (third from left, seated) took part in. (Courtesy of Caroline Cryar)

In 1930 Cedric Nutter and A. R. Woodson decided the county needed a golf course. Woodson's bank bought the land and sixty memberships were sold at $100 each. Mr. Nutter's gin crew from Dobbin helped to lay out the course. This clubhouse was built in 1935 at a cost of $7,000. The club still offers leisure to many in the area. (Courtesy of John and Sarah Gibson)

CHAPTER NINE

The Heritage of the Dream

Dreams such as those recorded here never really go away. We preserve them in pictures, in historical markers, in documents—but the true measure of a dream is in its continuity. The Montgomery County of today would not disappoint our early settlers. Its potential still draws many newcomers, some to live here and others to play. Lake Conroe and its resorts and communities, our forests and fine golf courses have made the county a major recreational area, the fifteenth in Texas in travel expenditure with over 6,000 visitors in 1995.

For those who come to stay they will find a diverse and dynamic economy. Tourism is a major base, bringing in over $4 million a year in tax revenues and providing over 2,600 jobs. Small businesses, commerce of all kinds, guarantees a job market with a low 4.2 percent unemployment rate. Our population, now around 225,000 is projected to be over 500,000 by the turn of the century.

The home of Ida Melissa Fowler Grogan now houses the Heritage Museum where the history of this county is preserved for all to learn about.

What draws these people here? Natural beauty, convenient access to roads and airports, medical care at our regional medical center, and schools (now including our own Montgomery College.) Our county airport, which offers both commercial and recreational flight opportunities, serves as a "reliever" for Houston Intercontinental, and even houses an Attack Helicopter unit of the Fifth Army Reserves.

The vision of such men as Austin and Dr. Stewart is kept alive here, both in the dreams of men like George Mitchell who has spurred amazing growth in the South County with The Woodlands and in our school children who can study the early dreams of our county, even experience the life our ancestors led here at the Heritage Museum. We hope this book has given each of you a clearer sense of this dream and your rich inheritance for years to come.

Ida Melissa Fowler Grogan, first wife of J. M. Grogan, died at age forty-five after bearing ten children and seeing much of the growth of Montgomery County.

The General Store, a hands on area, is a favorite.

At our summer Pioneer School children actually try their hands at aspects of pioneer life such as spinning and whitewashing.

Scout troops earn badges here.

Public school classes come to learn about Texas history from the Museum.

The young at heart, also a part of our heritage, come to learn, to teach us, or to reminisce.

I N D E X

Margaret Ann McCullough Simpson just missed being a true native of Montgomery County as she was born in Denton, Texas. on Christmas Day 1935, and only came here with her parents J. L. (Mac) McCullough and Eleanor in January of 1936. But her roots are here. She finished Conroe High School in 1953, went to North Texas State to study English and began her career in education in 1956. Her teaching posts have included Deer Park High School, Sam Houston State University, La Porte High School, and San Jacinto College in Houston where she spent thirty years as English professor and Division Head of Language Arts. During these years she earned her Ph.D. at Rice University and raised her children Deborah Kaye and Derrell, Jr.

Montgomery County drew her home in 1992 at retirement and here she enjoys a life full of her work at First Presbyterian Church in Conroe, at the Heritage Museum, and as director of the Pan-American Round Table. Of course, there's always time for card games with old and new friends and our new Montgomery College affords her a chance to continue her teaching.

The importance of heritage was instilled in her by her parents and she sees teaching and writing as a way of passing on that heritage to the future, to her children and to her granddaughter Miranda Alyse Gentile.

IN THE NAME

To all to whom these

I Mirabeau B Lamar PRESIDENT of

and in accordance with the STATUTES of SAID REPUBLIC, in such

Assignee his heirs or assign

of LAND, situated and described as follows:

In Spring Creek County, four mile

San Jacinto River, and about 25

Beginning at North West Corner of a

edge of a small prairie.

Thence North one thousand nine hundr

Thence East one thousand nine hundred

Thence South one thousand nine hundred

Thence West one thousand nine hundr

survey to the place of beginning.

Hereby relinquishing to him the said Edward Ma

in and to said LAND, heretofore held and possessed by the Govern

IN TESTIMONY WHEREOF I have caused the GREAT SEAL

DONE at the City of

One Thousand Eight Hundre

the Sixth

Thos Wm Ward   Commissioner

General Land Office.

I John Terr

certify, that the for

IN TESTIMONY WHEREOF I hereun

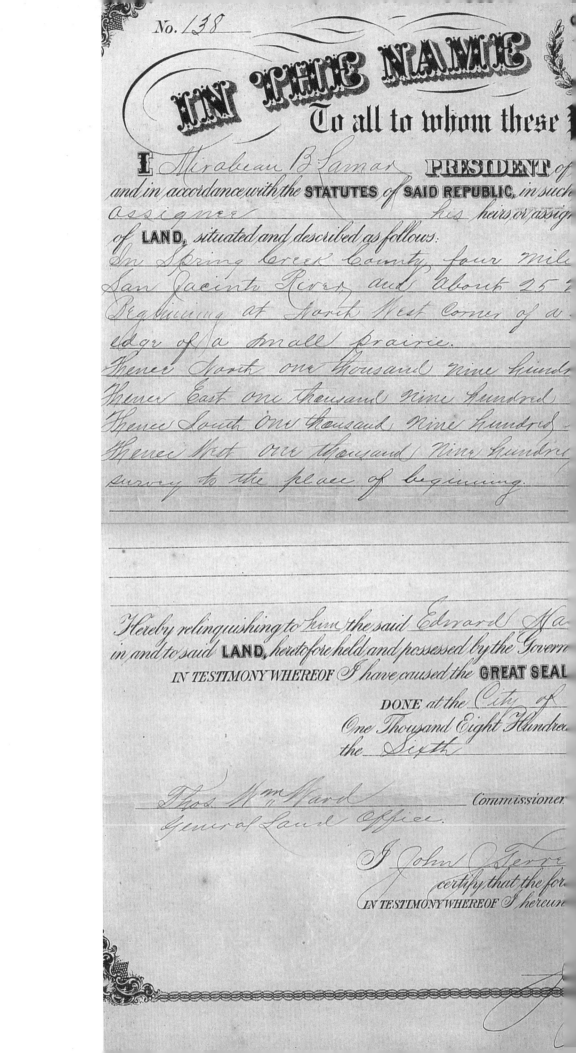